A Rich Gurlz Write
Book Collaborative Best Seller

PowHERed by
L. RENEE RICHARDSON, MBA
DR. JANET BENSON, RN, Ed.D
DR. CRYSTAL NEUMANN, DBA, MAED

UNLOVED

THE LEAH AND JACOB LOVE STORY

An exploration of love, betrayal, barrenness
and compensation by nine powHERful autHERS.

DEDICATED TO LEGENDARY LIFE
OF
DR. LAVERNE M. TAYLOR

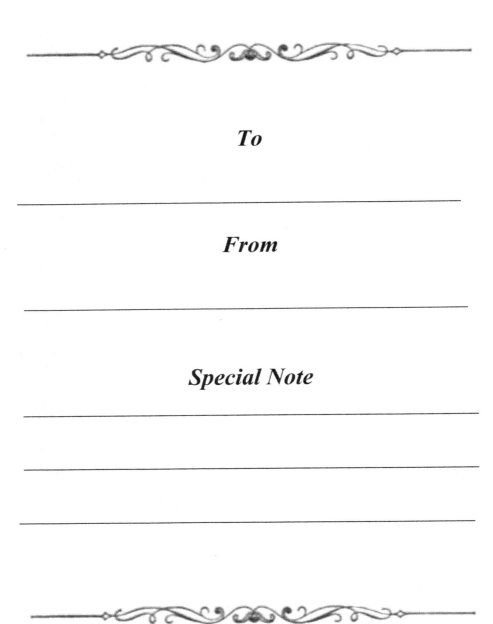

To

_____

From

_____

Special Note

_____

_____

_____

While the author has made every effort to provide accurate internet addresses at the time of publication, neither the publisher nor the author assumes any responsibility for errors or for changes that occur after publication.

Published in Chicago, Illinois by Rich Gurlz Club Inc.
John Hancock Center
875 North Michigan Avenue
31st Floor
Chicago, IL 60611
312.772.0406

Rich Gurlz Club Inc. is a wholly owned subsidiary of
Wealth and Riches Today, Inc.
Chicago, IL

Rich Gurlz Club Inc. titles may be purchased in bulk for
educational, business, fund-raising, or sales promotional use,
please email lrenee.richardson@wealthandrichestoday.com.

ISBN: 978 1 7366619 25

Library of Congress Cataloging in Publication
Printed in the United States of America

2021 First Edition

CHICAGO \\ ATLANTA \\ NEW YORK \\ CAPE TOWN\\ LAGOS\\ NEW DELHI

UNLOVED: The Leah and Jacob Love Story

*An Exploration of Love, Betrayal, Barrenness and
Compensation by Nine PowHERful
Rich Gurlz Write Books in 30 Days AutHERS*

*A Rich Gurlz Write Books in 30 Days Book
Collaborative*

CERTIFIED BY
WBENC/WEConnect INTERNATIONAL

W☼MEN™
OWNED

WWW.WOMENOWNEDLOGO.COM

Welcome to the Rich Gurlz Club, Inc. FranchiSHE!

Rich Gurlz Club Inc.

The Rich Gurlz Club Inc. is a wholly owned subsidiary of Wealth and Riches Today, Inc. headquartered in Chicago, IL (www.wealthandrichestoday.com) She is a global network of Christian women leadHERS in business, PastHERS in ministry, and Rich Corporate Gurlz. She is an Illinois corporation with a principal place of business in the John Hancock Center, 875 North Michigan Avenue in Chicago, IL overlooking lake Michigan, and Regional Corporate Offices and Dream CentHERS in Columbus, GA Co Work Center on the Riverfront.

The Rich Gurlz Club Inc. was birthed by FoundHER and SHE-E-O, L. Renee Richardson on her birthday, February 19, 2016. L. Renee tells the story about not being able to find another six-figure career, so she decided to follow her heart and create my own company designed for next-level women business leadHERs, PastHERs, and Rich Corporate Gurlz. Her company unleashes women into their destinies as Female FoundHERS and SHE-E-Os. Rich Gurlz are Proverbs 31-inspired, wealthy women who share their wealthy influence and resources for their families and to empower others. They are changing and protecting laws to reflect the Father's desire for women.

The Rich Gurlz Club Inc. underwrites causes benefiting young and seasoned women by donating a portion of every dollar earned to the Women of Vision and Destiny Ministries Worldwide, Inc. The ministry is celebrating more than 20 years of touching 1.5 million women worldwide. Rich Gurlz Club Inc. supports the two-year-old I AM Worth It Foundation, whose assignment is to raise $1 for every woman on the planet.

Rich Gurlz Write Books in 30 Days is the company's big, bodacious, and brilliant platform for Vision 20/21. The group is signing up over 1,001 Rich Gurlz Club Inc. AutHERs to share their HERstories with a GODstory. Sign up today to join this Rich Gurlz Club CommuniSHE at *RichGurlzWriteBooksin30Days.eventbrite.com*

Rich Color Gurlz Club Inc.

One June 1, 20/20 in the midst of racial turmoil in the U.S., I saw the need to incorporate a new company in Georgia, the Rich *Color* Gurlz Club Inc. for women of color business owners. It is headquartered at the Rich Gurlz Columbus, GA corporate headquarters and Dream CentHER at 1201 Front Avenue. Rich Color Gurlz Club empowers women of color to live beyond the boundaries of color and focus on excellence in the workforce, church and business worlds.

I became the 3rd highest ranking woman of color at the largest communications company in the world with 3,500 employees at the time, through the principles of prayer, strategic planning, and excellence. They say nice girls don't get the corner office, but I did! I was featured in numerous magazines and publications for my stellar corporate and business career. I have served in church leadHERship for 40 years and now own a global women's ministry and three global holding companies. Our biblical role models are the Proverbs 31 woman, The Widow Oil Tycoon in 2 Kings 4, Sheerah, Queen of Sheba, Lydia, Junia, and many more powerful women of God.

We would love for you to join us!
L. Renee
Pursue Your Dreams with Passion.
Dream in Billions.

9

Do you Love Our

Rich Gurlz Write Books in 30 Days Collaboratives?

We would love to hear your Feedback!

Email us your feedback on this book to
LRenee@wealthandrichestoday.com

and receive a FREE

UNLOVED: The Leah and Jacob Love Story Bookmark

A Heart Felt Dedication

This Rich Gurlz Write Books in 30 Days Collaborative is dedicated to L. Renee's incredible Mom and Matriarch Dr. Laverne M. Taylor whose legendary life impacted so many women. Dr. Laverne Taylor was a Fierce Nurse for 40 Years, a Missionary Evangelist Preacher, a Health Advocate, a Real Estate Mogul, a Philanthropist, PrayHER SlayHER, a CancHER OvercomHER. and Stroke FightHER who took her final exhale on September 11, 2021, Dr. Laverne M. Taylor Day at the beautiful age of 89. This day was the Global Book Launch of UNLOVED: The Leah and Jacob Love Story.

"When God realized that Leah was unloved, he opened her womb. But Rachel was barren."
Genesis 29:31 TM

#ILOVELEAH

A Message from WorldWide PastHER and Billionaire Visionnaire PublisHER L. Renee Richardson, MBA

Hello Gorgeous!

It has been an amazing journey since we began our Vision 20/21 quest to elevate the lives of women worldwide through our Rich Gurlz Club Inc.'s Publishing Company! We are the #1 Christian Women's Publishing House in the world. *UNLOVED: The Leah and Jacob Love Story* is the third book in our 20/21 **Rich Gurlz Write Books in 30 Days** trilogy. We pray that you get all three books which are available on Amazon: *God is My Portion: A PowHERful Look at Psalm 23 through the Eyes of 14 Women LeadHERs; Fashioned by God to Rule the World: A PowHERful Look at God's Original Design for Womankind by 11 Women LeadHERS;* and now this beauty you are holding in your powHERful hands. We have been blessed to create nearly 40 first time authors in just 90 Days of this year. Who does this but Jesus?

I self-published my first book *(Discover the Wealth that's in Your House)* on Amazon in November 2015 all by myself. Now we have a beautiful publishing team and Rich Gurlz Club Inc. AutHERS in 14 U.S. states and two continents, and we are still expanding. Our platform is **Rich Gurlz Write Books in 30 Days**. Our process is simple: you are trained to write your chapter in 30 days. You can visit RichGurlzWriteBooksin30Days.eventbrite.com to learn more and sign up.

We are excited you are joining us by reading book three *UNLOVED: The Leah and Rachel Love Story,* based on the biblical account found in Genesis 25-30. This title is a part of our Christian Women's Romance and Biblical Love Stories Division. In this book, we will unveil Jacob's story of family rejection as he seeks to take the family birthright and blessings away from his older brother Esau. Their struggle started in the womb. Each of their parents chose a different child to favor.

When the younger son, Jacob, won the birthright and blessings, he lost his relationship with his older brother Esau for a season. He leaves home to save his life and finds the love of his life at a dark place. Then he finds himself being used as a love pawn between sisters Leah and Rachel. He also had to share his love with two other women, his wives' handmaids, a total of four wives who birthed 13 children (12 sons and one daughter-known). In biblical circles as the children of Israel. Imagine being in love and romantically involved with four women. Today we call that baby momma drama.

Our Rich Gurlz Club Inc. Authors will explore the *Leah HERstory.* Leah spent her entire life looking for love in all the right places. She was not the prettiest young lady, but she was obedient to her father even in becoming Jacob's wife. She loved Jacob and kept seeking to gain his affections through having his children. Leah ended up terribly disappointed by her sister, dad, mom, and husband. She felt like a discarded and unwanted rose. Would she ever find true love?

God showed her His love through her desire to have children. When He saw she was unloved, He made her fruitful in childbearing. God always compensates us. Through this book, we will empower women to learn how much God loves us and compensates for our rejection! We will learn how to love ourselves.

HASHTAGS
Our book hashtag is #ILOVELEAH. Please put this #hashtag in all your social media posts.
OUR RICH GURLZ CLUB INC. BEAUTIQUE
WWW.WEALTHANDRICHESTODAY.COM/SHOP

L. Renee LuXury Spa WeekendHERs FUNraisers are held for our Female FoundHERS and SHE-E-Os in Columbus, GA.
LReneeLuXuryOctober.eventbrite.com

A Letter from our Signature Editor
Dr. Janet Benson
RN, BSN, MS, M.Ed, Ed.D, PEL-CSN

Dear Rich Gurl,

If you've ever felt unloved, despite using every tool in your personal love arsenal to achieve a successful relationship, this book is for you. You will read about some very blessed and significant people in the Bible, whom God chose to use for His will. There is jealousy, anger, disobedience, disrespect, sorrow, forgiveness, and love, permeating every page of the book. There are times you will see yourself in these pages. Perhaps you'll learn what you should or should not have done in your last relationship and how you could have made it better. It is our hope that whether this book improves your current relationship or causes you to end it, you will discover where true love starts.

God is the Creator and Sustainer of love, which is evident in each of our lives. We have made mistakes and bad choices, even deliberately being disobedient and yet, He continues to bless us. My prayer is that you find true love, first in a relationship with the Father and then with yourself.

Be well.
Dr. Janet Benson, Signature AutHER

A Letter from our Signature Editor
Dr. Crystal Neumann
DBA, MAED, MBA, BBA, BS, MH, CHt, RYT 200

Dear Rich Gurl,

Love is a universal experience and can be felt in a variety of forms—true love, unrequited love, love for your family, unconditional love, and more. This is why our souls are touched whenever we listen to a ballad or read a love poem. Yet, when emotions go unchecked, we can also see love in unhealthy forms, ranging from jealousy to anger. Perhaps we may see the lines blurred from love to hate.

This book tells the story of Leah and Jacob from the perspectives of several wonderful women. Our life experiences, wisdom, and raw feelings have been brought together to produce this collaboration. There are so many incredible stories shared here; I know you will identify with at least one. In love, we find contentment and what is means to be human. In life, most of us have had the privilege of finding someone we can talk to for hours, or simply enjoy their presence without feeling bored. We can tell this person anything, free of judgement, and simply be who we are. This person's smile makes our day. We may not see them for years and can pick right up where we left off. Consider that for someone else, *we* are that person. Our connections with others create beautiful, loving relationships. It is because of love, and for love, that

God created us. Enjoy as you read about God's unique expression of love through Leah, Rachel, and Jacob.

Sincerely,
Crystal Neumann, Signature AutHER

We are looking for women who love to write!

It's time to tell your HERstory with a GODstory.

Leave a Legacy.

Learn more and sign up today!

We have 50 new books coming out in Vision 20/22. We start writing in October 20/21.

Become a Rich Gurlz Write Books in 30 Days AutHER.

Sign up today! Visit

RichGurlzWriteBooksin30Days.eventbrite.com

UNLOVED: The Leah and Jacob Love Story
Our Fabulous HERstory with a GODstory

Chapter 1: Jacob's Story: Sibling Womb Wars, Fight for the Birthright
(Genesis 25:19-34)
Flossie Berry

Chapter 2: Jacob's Mother Plots for the Blessing, A Mother's Send Off
(Genesis 27:1-17; 42-46)
L. Renee Richardson

Chapter 3: A Mother and Father's Instructions for Wife-Selection
(Genesis 27:46; Genesis 28:1-2, 5-9)
Dr. Janet Benson

Chapter 4: Capturing a Man's Heart: A Woman's Kiss that Makes a Man Cry
(Genesis 29:1-13)
Dr. Crystal Neumann

Chapter 5: A Tale of Two Sisters: Leah and Rachel
(Genesis 29:16-30)
Dr. Sheriolyn Curry aka Dr. Joy

Chapter 6: Leah's Misery: Now Jacob Will Love Me
(Genesis 29: 31-32)
Latoia Russell-Williams

Chapter 7: God's Compensation for Rejection: Leah's Fertile Years
(Genesis 29:33-35)
Katrina Washington

Chapter 8: The Sisters' Big Rivalry: Rachel's Jealousy of Leah
(Genesis 30:1-2; 6-8; 14-21)
Sharyn G. Dyer

Chapter 9: Jacob: A Pawn in Women's Love Games
(Genesis 30:3-5; 9-21)
Sheila Dudley

Chapter 1

Jacob's Story: Sibling Womb Wars, Fight for the Birthright
Flossie Berry, AS, BS-Biblical Studies, BS Management

Flossie's HERstory

Flossie Berry is an evangelist, prayer warrior, a worshipper, motivational and inspirational speaker, innovator, thought leader, teacher, change agent, youth advocate, entrepreneur, author, a fashion blogger, mentor, and preacher. One of her favorite scriptures is Isaiah 40:30-31, "Even the youths shall faint and be weary, and the young men shall utterly fall: But they that wait upon the Lord shall renew their strength; they shall mount up with wings as eagles; they shall run, and not be weary; and they shall walk, and not faint."

Flossie currently serves as an evangelist and team lead over the Single Women's Ministry at The Kingdom Church, Love Fellowship Tabernacle, under the leadership of Bishop Hezekiah X. Walker. As a young girl, Flossie enjoyed writing songs, and creating and performing in productions with friends, participating in sports and hosting various events. With a passion for singing and music, she set out to start a singing group with her sisters when they were very young. The group evolved and was called "The Berry Sisters". Her love for music afforded her the opportunity to become a member of the Grammy Award-winning choir Hezekiah Walker and the Love Fellowship Crusade.

Flossie is a pastor's kid (P.K.), who was born and raised in Albany, NY. She eventually moved to New York City where her father, the late Pastor Joseph L. Berry, was called to pastor at The Church of the Lord of Lords, a ministry originally founded by his parents, Pastor John and Elizabeth Berry.

Flossie always had her sights set on moving to the "Big Apple," especially because of her love for fashion. Upon graduating from high school, she moved to New York and attended St. John's University where she received her Bachelor of Science Degree in Business Management. She attended during the time when St. John's Basketball team, the Redmen, were champions under the leadership of Coach Lou Carnesecca. The team boasted players including Chris Mullen, Mark Jackson, and Bill Wennington.

As a motivational and inspirational speaker, Flossie seeks to empower, uplift, and elevate women, men, and youth. Flossie is an advocate for young people and has shown immeasurable love towards them. Her dedication to the youth led to the formation of MPact, a holistic entrepreneur program created to mentor and develop purpose-driven youth leaders with a focus on young men. MPact aspires to build an "I can do it" generation by encouraging our youth to tap into their intrinsic ability to create. The organization's foundational scripture is Philippians 4:13, "I can do all things through Christ which strengthens me." As a change agent, Flossie seeks to transform, inspire, and influence individuals to live intentionally. One of her more inherent characteristics is the innate ability to assist others in unmasking and developing their inner gifts and talents. Flossie recently received her Life Coach and Mentor certification through the Destiny Academy Training program.

Since God has given her a heart to empower women, Flossie is establishing an organization entitled Facets of a Women, which seeks to unearth the hidden gems within each of us, that make us "diamonds in the rough". The challenge that many women face today is the inability to find space to unveil their authentic inner selves, and the lack of exposure to resources that would enable them to make better life choices. Facets of a Women was birthed to form a community that offers a place for women to share their powerful stories, while providing them with tools to help build, rebuild, or reinvent their career, business, finances, ministry, family, health, education, or social and mental wellbeing. Flossie is currently a co-host on SoulSistas, a social media platform designed to highlight women in ministry.

Although she works in the in the beauty industry, Flossie is also an entrepreneur; she is the CEO of an online clothing boutique, FloJo NY. As a stylist, image consultant, and a fashion/lifestyle concierge, Flossie's brand is comprised of unique, quality apparel and accessories that provide value to distinctive women and individuals. It is her desire that people be inspired and empowered through beauty and fashion. To capture this, she recently coined the quote, "Be Stylish, Be Unique, Be You".

Flossie currently lives in Queens, NY and is a proud mother of her son, Marquis, who resides in Arizona. She is pursuing a master's degree. She has written her chapter of *Unloved* in loving memory of her father, her hero and best friend, who exemplified true love toward his wife and family.

Chapter 1
Jacob's Story: Sibling Womb Wars, Fight for the Birthright
(Genesis 25:19-34)
Flossie Berry

I have been given the task of introducing the writings of the book *Unloved, the Leah and Jacob Story*. In the midst of a pandemic, I am blessed to have received the opportunity to collaborate with a collection of beautiful authors in writing this incredible book. I invite you to walk with me as I unveil the story of sibling rivalry between Jacob and Esau. It took a while for me to grasp the topic and understand how it fits within my own story. As far as I've known, there had been no sibling rivalry in our family. I had a father who truly loved his six children, and who adored his wife. As a matter of fact, my dad would often quote Ephesians 5:25, "Husbands, love your wives, even as Christ also loved the church, and gave himself for it." This is a motto that he worked hard to emulate throughout his life.

In this chapter I will share how my story loosely compares to Jacob and Esau's narrative. As I delve into my assigned scripture, Genesis 25:19-34, I will alternate between discussing what was occurring during the biblical time the scripture illustrates, and what was in happening my own life. The biblical narrative discusses twin brothers who fight over their family's birthright. I thought it would be good to first give you several definitions of the word "birthright". According to Wikipedia, birthright means right, privilege, or possession to which a person is entitled to by birth. Now the biblical terminology of birthright (bekorah in Hebrew) deals with both position and inheritance. By birthright, the firstborn son inherited the leadership of the family and the judicial authority of his father. Deuteronomy 21:17 says that he was also entitled to a double portion of the paternal inheritance. In receiving the birthright, the firstborn would become the head of the family, and take charge of the family and the family property. His responsibility would also extend to the welfare of the younger brothers, the widow, and any unmarried sisters. In reading these definitions, by all accounts, the birthright rightfully belonged to Esau since he was the eldest twin.

The story commences with Isaac, who is now 40 years old,

taking Rebekah to be his lawful wedded wife. Now that they were married, Isaac and Rebekah were trying very hard to conceive a child but to no avail. They did not have the choices like we do today of introducing invitro fertilization or surrogacy into their birthing plan. What I thought was remarkable about this story is that Isaac, as a man and as her husband, did not give up. He understood his assignment as the priest of his home. So, he took authority and the reigns as the priest and began praying and petitioning God to open her womb. Our all-seeing God who possesses omnipotent power heard his prayer, opened her womb and Rebekah was finally able to do what she was unable to do for 20 years, conceive a child.

I must pause here because as a woman I thought this was such a compelling moment. To see in this powerful story where the priest of your home intercedes, or shall we say, goes to bat on your behalf by crying out to God. This is not a story that you hear shared often amongst women. What was even more incredible about this story is that she was not only pregnant, but with twins which she named Jacob and Esau. Esau's name meant hairy, and Jacob's name meant usurper or supplanter. Can you imagine how overjoyed these parents must have been having the ability to finally conceive and with Isaac being able to see this miraculous event unfold at the age sixty? Take a minute to allow this to sink into your psyche. It took 20 whole years for the blessing to manifest in their lives. It is wonderful to remember and to note that although the promise may have been delayed, it was not denied.

As a new mom-to-be today, you might find yourself dealing with things like overeating, sleeping more often than you would like, having overwhelming cravings for combinations of things that might seem weird to you like pickles, broccoli, and ice cream. Now as a new mom herself, Rebekah was dealing with something totally different. She became nervous when she realized that the two babies she was carrying seemed like they were wrestling inside her womb. This caused her to implore God for answers. God revealed to her that the two babies were two nations that were growing inside of her womb and that the older child was going to serve the younger one. This news could not have been easy for her to digest. It had to have placed her in an awkward and uneasy position knowing that her oldest child would not rightfully inherit his birthright. Having firsthand knowledge of this information makes you wonder what her frame of mind must have been. Who would she decide to nurture more? Which baby could quite possibly receive a deficit of her love?

Identity Crisis

Jacob said, "First, swear to me." And he did it. On oath Esau traded away his rights as the firstborn. Jacob gave him bread and the stew of lentils. He ate and drank, got up and left. That's how Esau shrugged off his rights as the firstborn.

—Genesis 25:33-34 TM

The Merriam-Webster dictionary describes an identity crisis as a "personal psychosocial conflict especially in adolescence that involves confusion about one's social role and often a sense of loss of continuity to one's personality." The stage of psychosocial development in which the identity crisis may occur is called the identity cohesion vs. role confusion. During this stage, adolescents are faced with physical growth, sexual maturity, and integrating ideas about themselves and about what others may think of them.

In our story, we see that not only was the oldest twin, Esau, suffering from an identity crisis but he also suffered from a recognition crisis. He did not realize who he was and that became apparent when he sold his birthright, as well as his rights as the firstborn, for a bowl of stew. He traded something that was priceless for something of so little value. It is important to note that having an identity crisis can distort your purpose, cause you to question your sense of self, and ultimately lead you to make erroneous decisions in life. In Christ we were also chosen, having been predestined according to the plan of Him who works out everything in conformity with the purpose of his will, according to Ephesians 1:11 NIV.

Born and raised in, Albany, NY, I was the first daughter born to the union of Pastor Joseph and First Lady Flossie Berry. I grew up in a family of three boys and three girls causing us to earn the nickname "The Berry Bunch," which was a play on "The Brady Bunch," for those of you who are familiar with the 1970's sitcom. I can honestly say that before my younger sisters were born, growing up around my brothers made me a little rough around the edges. So, between the formative ages of five to seven years old, I climbed trees, played cops and robbers, and often innocently followed my brother around trying to mimic what they did. It got so bad, I began saying "I'm a boy," and would find myself getting upset when others replied, "No, you are a girl." I pondered this as I got older and realized how confusing this type of thinking could have been for me, especially since it occurred at such an impressionable age. Now, there were others around me that understood that I was just being what they called a "tom boy". I can assure you that as a young child, although I may have displayed uninformed tendencies, I was not suffering from an identity crisis.

It is pertinent as parents to recognize what's brewing inside of our children, whether it is curiosity or the various gifts your child may possess. It is crucial that you recognize this early, give them the right tools to be informed and work on assisting them in developing those talents. You want them to identify who they are and to know what they possess early on in life, so that they are less likely to experience an identity crisis. It is wonderful to know that I was chosen and that my life was predestined by God. So, no matter the many roadblocks I experienced during my childhood, the Holy Spirit was there to cover and steer me in the right direction. He had a plan for my life.

The Importance of Education in my Family

Growing up, my parents always made us feel like we could accomplish anything. Education was an intricate tool that was infused into the life of our family. For example, upon my graduating and moving on to the fourth grade, my mom took it upon herself to go before the Board of Education to fight on my behalf so that I could attend a magnet school outside of my district that had an Academically Talented program for gifted children. It was important to them that we all had the opportunity to obtain a college education, especially since my dad only had a sixth-grade education and my mom had obtained her high school diploma. What was even more extraordinary is my dad never allowed his lack of education to handicap him. He was able to develop and educate himself through his love of reading and by seeking the wisdom and knowledge of God. Our home was filled with all kinds of books like various brands of encyclopedias, non-fiction books and autobiographies, magazines; you name it and we probably had it in our library. I am sure there were times when he entered a room of scholars and felt inadequate, but there is a wonderful passage of scripture, James 1:5 KJV, that says, "If any of you lack wisdom, let him ask of God, that giveth to all men liberally, and upbraideth not; and it shall be given him." I must say that my dad truly possessed a wealth of wisdom. I realized as I got older that life is not predicated on how educated you are, your position or status, whether you are rich or poor, or if you are the eldest or the youngest child in your family. I learned that whatever God's plan is for your life, or whatever promises He has made to you are destined to come to pass.

It was in that vein, that I knew I wanted to make my parents proud. So, upon moving to New York, I continued my education by attending one of the top colleges in the country, St. John's University. I then reached a milestone achievement by becoming the first one within my immediate family to obtain a bachelor's degree.

What's in a Name?

The first was born so covered with reddish hair that one would think he was wearing a fur coat! So they called him "Esau." Then the other twin was born with his hand on Esau's heel! So they called him Jacob (meaning "Grabber"). Isaac was sixty years old when the twins were born.

—Genesis 25: 25-26 TLB

When it comes to names, they are considered a part of our identity. Your name can carry deep, personal, cultural, and historical connections. A person's name is the greatest correlation to their identity and individuality. Some might deem it as the most important word in the world to individuals that carry weight. That is why it is very important that when we choose a name for a child, we choose wisely. A person is or can become their name. In this story, one of the twins was named Esau which meant "hairy," and the other twin was named Jacob which meant "supplanter or trickster". Jacob got an opportunity to prove his name by tricking his brother Esau into selling him his birthright for a bowl of stew. Remember historically and biblically the birthright was given to the firstborn son who then earns the leadership role and the inheritance of the family.

While doing a little research, I happened upon the breakdown of my name, and I thought it was fascinating. I was not fond of my name until I got older and learned to appreciate it. I now have a newfound love for my name. Take a moment to read the next several sentences that express the meaning of my name "Flossie": kind, home-loving, hospitable, and friendly, takes on responsibility well, a good organizer of social affairs, has compassion for others, practical, yet idealistic and intuitive, capable of selfless devotion to someone you love, frank, methodical, and believes in the law, systems, and order. My name also means dependable, very down-to-earth, well-grounded, always looking for meaningful work, a career where I can take pride in my work and do the best job I can; I desire to build a protected and secure environment at home and at work. Flossie means very persuasive in achieving goals and gaining objectives, very detailed and well-organized and possesses great organizational skills, at times I may appear stubborn and overly critical, but my practical approach to life and productivity makes me one of the most beneficent members of the community.

Now for those of you who may not know me this will mean nothing to you, but for those of you who do, you may find that to be a pretty close description of me.

Daddy's Little Girl is also an Heir

The babies jostled each other within her, and she said, "Why is this happening to me?" So she went to inquire of the Lord. 23 The Lord said to her, "Two nations are in your womb, and two peoples from within you will be separated; one people will be stronger than the other, and the older will serve the younger." 28 Isaac, who had a taste for wild game, loved Esau, but Rebekah loved Jacob.
— Genesis 25: 22-23;28

The definition of daddy's little girl in the Urban Dictionary is a girl (adult or child) who has a strong bond with her father. In our story, since we are dealing with sons, we see that Esau had a strong bond with his father Isaac and Jacob had a strong bond with his mother Rebekah. I am under the impression that when Rebekah was told by God that there were two nations growing inside of her womb and the youngest child would one day rule the oldest, she began to set things in motion by plotting and taking matters into her own hands so that Jacob could obtain the birthright. Sometimes, we make the mistake of taking matters into our own hands believing we can help God along, as if He needs our help. Probing in an area where you don't belong or where you don't have the expertise can bring about confusion, and even destruction, which can interfere with, delay, or destroy the promises God has for you.

I, too, had a very strong bond with my father. I considered him to be my best friend, hero, mentor, counselor, guide, encourager, influencer, rock, and he was my pastor. Our relationship was such that I could confide in him about almost anything. I was that overzealous kid who would follow behind my dad wherever he went. So, when he would leave the house to run errands whether it was to the corner store, Dunkin Donuts, the hardware store, a drive by at Stewarts Ice Cream shop, grabbing a newspaper from the newsstand, visiting a friend or family member, or stopping by the church, I would try to make it my business to go with him. Now that's not to say that he always wanted me to go, but he often gave in when I batted my eyes and pouted. Little did I know, that by doing this and more, I was being trained by my dad and others for an even greater purpose.

My father began to slowly involve me in many family and ministry affairs. I considered it wonderful and incredible that he respected my opinion on various issues. Not only was I being set in alignment to become a leader, but I was also strongly looked to as an example for my siblings and family. In Ephesians1:11TPT it states that through our union with Christ we too have been claimed by God as his own inheritance. Before we were even born, He gave us our destiny, that we would fulfill the plan of God who always accomplishes every purpose and plan in His heart. I wanted to remind you that through it all it wasn't important to my dad that I was not the oldest nor the male child. This bought back to my memory some of the challenges my dad faced when he was installed over the ministry as pastor. Not everyone agreed with this decision, and others may have felt that this role was supposed to be given to them. Either way my father gracefully walked in his position, although he faced challenges along the way, because this was ultimately the plan of God.

As I write this chapter, I am reminded of the plethora of expectations that was placed on my life as a P.K., whether it was from family, the ministry, or friends. I was like a second mother to both of my younger sisters, so they pretty much became a staple wherever I went. With regard to the ministry, I had the assignment of holding a myriad of positions like church secretary, minister, Sunday school teacher, choir director, and more. I often felt the weight of that responsibility, which at times was overwhelming as I navigated through life because I always believed that there was an expectation for me to be all things to all people. Living the life of a P.K., especially being a daughter, you were often scrutinized and held to a much higher standard than others. This contributed to me feeling like I had to be that perfect individual, to be a role model, to sacrifice and be there for others, to be selfless, to be that "yes gal," to live a life where I had to dot every "i" and cross every "t". As I am sure you may realize, being put in this situation could be overwhelming and mentally exhausting for anyone. In truth, life was not always easy for me, and I did not always handle things perfectly.

Through it all, I came to realize that not only was I my father's daughter, but I was also a daughter of God. The Scripture states, "And, I will be a Father to you, and you will be my sons and daughters, the Lord Almighty," 2 Corinthians 6:18 KJV. I am the beloved of the Father, and in His eyes, it does not matter whether I am male or female because I am worthy of the inheritance of my father. I am reminded of a special story in the Bible regarding the five daughters of Zelophehad in which they stood before Moses and asked for their father's inheritance because their father had no sons. Moses inquired of God who replied that the daughters should indeed possess the inheritance of their father (Numbers 27:1-11). I am excited to know that being born into the Kingdom of God gives me access as His daughter and allows me to know that just like my natural father:

I am accepted by Him
I can always come to Him because His love is unconditional
He always hears me
He has my back
He won't walk out on me or leave me
I can look up to Him, respect Him, and honor Him

They Love me, They Love me Not, They Love me

Little did I know growing up, that there was somewhat of a wall being created between my brothers and me as well as my sisters. We were raised in a loving family household that was not perfect. My parents loved us and showed love to all their children. It just so happened that because us girls were around them more, the love was being presented as one-sided. We (the girls) had given our lives to Christ and were often around my parents when we had our weekly church services, which was three to four times a week. We attended preaching engagements, traveled to conferences and conventions, went on church picnics, visited guest ministries, went to revivals, and church anniversaries, so we had the opportunity to be around my parents quite a bit. In my brothers' eyes, unbeknownst to me and my sisters, the church was not always viewed in a good light. The very thing that we and our parents had in common, a relationship with God, was also the very thing that brought a wedge between our relationship with our brothers. So instead of bringing about inclusion, it bought about separation.

Over the years, this caused communication issues to arise at times because my brothers may have felt that favoritism was shown to me and my sisters. Ultimately, I think maybe they felt that they weren't loved as much as their sisters because the church and their sisters seemed to take precedence in their parents' lives. Sometimes children can compete to get noticed through other mechanisms, such as addictive behaviors, because they are not receiving their parents' attention. I know this is not just our story but the story of many others who grew up in a P.K. household, or any other household. I am pretty sure if my parents knew then what is known now, they would have found ways to incorporate and embrace my brothers in all that they were doing.

Could this have been the miseducation of the Church? To help, we often quoted scriptures like 2 Corinthians 6;14, "Be ye not unequally yoked together with unbelievers: for what fellowship hath righteousness with unrighteousness? and what communion hath light with darkness?" or "Wherefore come out from among them, and be ye separate, saith the Lord, to come out from amongst them and be ye separate saith the Lord," 2 Corinthians 6:17.

Little did we know, all this did was bring about a separation in our family that was not intended by God because God is love. Could we have missed the mark? Did we err by misquoting these scriptures? Did we unknowingly preach separation instead? Did some of our brothers and sisters miss out because we didn't know how to embrace and incorporate their gifts and talents? As stated earlier, this was not something that was intentionally imputed toward my brothers because my parents loved them. Why do we demonize one child and show favor to the other when God loves us unconditionally? I thought Romans 2:11 TM might best fit this conversation.

It states, "For God treats everyone the same." I feel it is crucial to remember that while you are building a business, ministry, or an empire that you embrace your family and allow them to take part in some way so that no one feels excluded while you pursue your purpose.

We Have an Advocate

Once when Jacob was cooking some stew, Esau came in from the open country, famished. He said to Jacob, "Quick, let me have some of that red stew! I'm famished!" (That is why he was also called Edom. Jacob replied, "First sell me your birthright." "Look, I am about to die," Esau said. "What good is the birthright to me?" But Jacob said, "Swear to me first." So he swore an oath to him, selling his birthright to Jacob. Then Jacob gave Esau some bread and some lentil stew. He ate and drank, and then got up and left. So Esau despised his birthright.
—Genesis 25:29-34

Now in our story, we see that Esau placed himself in a negligent position by selling his birthright for stew. He came home famished and worn out from hunting but made a major decision, or shall I say a mistake, that would change the trajectory of his life and lineage. I had graduated from college and was excited about utilizing my education and looked forward to building my career in business management. So, you can imagine how devastated I was when life took a wrong turn for me. I found out that I was pregnant. Yes, pregnant. I must admit, that finding out this news initially put me in a dark place. I found myself overwhelmed with guilt, embarrassment, shame and of course, I had let a myriad of people down including my parents but more importantly, God. Although my decision had initially put me in a bad emotional and spiritual state, I was determined to not allow it to deter me from what God had destined for my life.

I came to understand that if you do not take time to carefully think matters through, one wrong decision could cause a major disruption in your life, including possibly losing everything. I also learned that it is extremely important to treasure and value all that God has given you. Through this process, I felt it was imperative that I own up to my mistakes. So yes, the decision I made caused me to initially be estranged from my Father, but this scripture became my saving grace, "My dear children, I write this to you so that you will not sin. But if anybody does sin, we have an advocate with the Father—Jesus Christ, the Righteous One. He is the atoning sacrifice for our sins, and not only for ours but also for the sins of the whole world" 1 John 2: 1-2 NIV.

My Best Friend Received His Wings

"He will wipe every tear from their eyes. There will be no more death or mourning or crying or pain, for the old order of things has passed away."

—*Revelation 21:4 NIV*

As things in my life began to evolve and move forward, I found myself not only being a mom to my wonderful son but also becoming a very busy woman. I was serving at my church, The Church of the Lord of Lords, singing with Hezekiah Walker and the Love Fellowship Crusade Choir, and singing on circuits with the Berry Sisters, as well as having several preaching engagements. While life was moving forward, my mom received news that my dad had cancer. We were a close-knit family, so this news was shocking and a devastating blow to us and to our church. So, we began to do what we knew worked—we prayed. We fasted, prayed, interceded, and cried out to God on behalf of my father and our pastor, and we enlisted others to do the same. All of this took place within a span of about six months.

Then the unthinkable happened. On a chilly day in March, we received the news that my dad lost his battle with cancer. What do you do when you lose your father, mentor, hero, best friend, and pastor all at once? His passing caused the memory of the loss of my brother Joseph, dad's namesake, who was musically talented and preceded him in death due to alcoholism. I was overwhelmed and numb by this loss and there were times when I felt like I was walking around in a fog. I would say I was going through periods of grief, shock, denial, pain, guilt, and even anger. I did not know it at the time but realized later that I was also going through depression. Having your father and your man of God gone from your life at the same time was a double whammy for me.

During my time of grief, I was able to put on a facade where outwardly I functioned around my family, my peers, and my church family, while inwardly feeling deep loss. There were days when I laid in bed crying, feeling angry, brokenhearted, and inquiring of a Sovereign God, why? When attending church services, I felt different, somewhat uncomfortable, and mentally drained. I had lost some of my passion and had never quite settled back into the rhythm of things. I knew the Word said that to be absent from the body was to be present with the

Lord, but what I did not know was that the absence of my father here on earth would

hurt me so deeply.

After wallowing in my sorrows for a period, I finally began feeling like I was coming up out of my bubble. I must admit that this was not easy for me, but I was able to navigate and get through this tough time in my life because of the Word of God and the power of prayer. I was reminded in Psalms 34:18 NIV, "The Lord is close to the brokenhearted and saves those
who are crushed in spirit."

Grief Stricken

"The thief cometh not, but for to steal, and to kill, and to destroy: I am come that they might have life, and that they might have it more abundantly."

—John 10:10 KJV

I did not know it until I experienced my father's death that grief can throw you into a tailspin and it can even threaten to throw you off course. What do I mean? It can confuse you, interrupt your day-to-day living, throw you off your path, change your thought pattern, mislead you, or have a tumultuous effect on your emotions. I realized during the process of my healing that my passion had dimmed for some things. It was like having an individual that was excellent at playing basketball one day and the next day they no longer had the passion for or interest in playing sports. Sadly, because my dad was not healed here on earth, I felt myself at times questioning my faith. Without even realizing it, I had allowed the enemy to seep in through the door of my grief, and place doubt in my belief system. Imagine, seeing and hearing testimonies of others being healed by the power of God and then seeing your father die of cancer knowing that God is Jehovah Rapha.

It was Satan's optimal plan to cause me to lose faith and to ultimately forfeit being an heir. It was in God's divine plan that I live and continue to declare the works of the Lord. It states in Romans 8:1 TPT, "And since we are his true children, we qualify to share all his treasures, for indeed, we are heirs of God himself. And since we are joined to Christ, we also inherit all that he is and all that he has. We will experience being co-glorified with him provided that we accept his

39

sufferings as our own."

In a Barren State

"Isaac was forty years old when he married Rebekah daughter of Bethuel the Aramean from Paddan Aram and sister of Laban the Aramean. Isaac prayed to the Lord on behalf of his wife, because she was childless. The Lord answered his prayer, and his wife Rebekah became pregnant."

—Genesis 25: 20-21 NIV

When we look at our story, we see that Rebekah was dealt a devastating blow. She was married to Isaac and found out that she was barren or unable to bear children. Barrenness is the inability or ability of man and woman to procreate. You must understand that children are considered one of the greatest blessings of God, so imagine the mother of a promised child being barren for twenty years.

I am sure that this caused her shame, anxiety, pain, embarrassment, and dismay. Being able to procreate was and is still considered a blessing. So, her husband Isaac, through a deep, intensive prayer, entreated God to open her womb. They were totally dependent on God, the Giver of life, to perform a miracle for their heir to be born. The Lord heard and answered their prayer and Rebekah became pregnant.

My son and I moved to Dallas, TX about 10 years after my dad had gone on to be with the Lord. One day when my son and I were heading in to work, I began to feel dizzy and faint and could hardly move. The ambulance was called, and I was rushed to the hospital. A lot of tests were run, and it was determined that I had several large fibroids that needed to be removed. Normally, these are uterine fibroids that are non-cancerous clumps of tissue and muscle on the walls of the uterus. What I failed to realize is that my body had been hemorrhaging for quite some time. I had lost so much blood over a point in time that it now required me to have a blood transfusion. I needed to be infused with eight pints of blood before any procedures could be performed. Although the blood loss was something that happened over a period time, the doctors were amazed that I was still able to walk around. I was considered a walking miracle and did not even know it.

After taking me through a plethora of tests, I was relayed some devastating news. I was advised by my doctor that I would need to have a hysterectomy. For those of you who may not know what that is, a hysterectomy is a surgical operation to remove all or part of a woman's uterus. My head was reeling, and I was in total shock by the news that I received from the doctors. Having to get a blood transfusion was one thing and then being told that your reproductive organ was being removed was something totally different. It felt like I had been given a death sentence.

Even though this was a travesty for me, this is a procedure that is performed all too many times on women, especially women of color. Removing it means you go directly into menopause, and you are unable to get pregnant. Losing the capacity for this in a single procedure can be a lot to process for some women. It was a lot for me to process.

Through my experience, I had to remember that God can bring life to those barren places in your life. I am ecstatic to know that through my experiences and life journey whether it was at times feeling unloved, lonely, experiencing loss, or even going through grief, it was amazing to know that God was always there. His Word says that He would never leave me nor forsake me. Romans 8:35 in The Message Bible states, "Do you think anyone is going to be able to drive a wedge between us and Christ's love for us? There is no way! Not trouble, not hard times, not hatred, not hunger, not homelessness, not bullying threats, not backstabbing, not even the worst sins listed in Scripture."

Chapter 2

Jacob's Mother Plots for the Blessing, A Mother's Send Off
L. Renee Richardson, MBA
WorldWide PastHER, ChairHERman of the Board, L. Renee Richardson, MBA

L. Renee's HERstory

L. Renee Richardson, MBA, is the FoundHER/ChairHERman of the Board of three global corporations: Women of Vision and Destiny Ministries Worldwide, Inc., Wealth and Riches Today Inc., and the I AM Worth It Foundation Inc., headquartered in Chicago, all of which she built within the last two decades. L. Renee oversees global teams in North America, Asia, and Africa. Wealth and Riches Today, Inc. is a WBENC Certified Women Owned Enterprise, placing it in the top .12 percent of the 13.2 million women-owned businesses in the United States. L. Renee operates corporate offices and Dream CentHERS out of two prime and upscale locations: Chicago's John Hancock Center overlooking Michigan Avenue and Columbus, GA in the CoWork Center on the riverfront.

For more than 40 years, L. Renee has served at top levels of leadership in the corporate, ministry/church/kingdom, and entrepreneurship arenas. Throughout her Christian journey, L. Renee served under the following pastors, Bishop Luther C. Anderson, Bishop Prince James, Bishop A.C. Richards, Bishop Dr. Horace E. Smith, Bishop D. Rayford Bell, Bishop Warren J. Hoard, Dr. Bill and Veronica Winston, and Bishop L.D. Skinner and held in leadership positions in the Living Witnesses of the Apostolic Faith, Pentecostal Assemblies of the World and the Pentecostal Churches of the Apostolic Faith International.

After serving in senior church leadership for 24 years, the Lord called her to lead her own ministry, Women of Vision and Destiny Ministries Worldwide, Inc. (WOVD) which she started in 2000, through a divine impartation by Convening Apostle Dr. Ron Cottle (www.roncottle.com). In November of that year, L. Renee was visiting her parents in Columbus, GA, and attended a workshop where Dr. Cottle was teaching on Moses at the burning bush, purpose, and destiny— terms with which she was unfamiliar. After the class, she asked Dr. Cottle to pray for her. Instead, he said he was going to impart. She remembers hearing him say that the anointing that was on him he would place on her. He had everyone in the room point their hands to her as he imparted. In that moment her whole world changed. L. Renee returned home to Chicago and WOVD was birthed the next week. Fifteen years later in 2015, L. Renee was released into full-time ministry. In 2017, women across the world began to ask for WOVD to be made available in their communities. In response, L. Renee designed a 10-year Vision 20/25 to build 57 women's centers and 10 LOVED Academies with the goal of touching the lives of 4 billion women. After L. Renee had moved back to Columbus, GA in 2019 to care for her aging parents, Dr. Ron Cottle ordained L. Renee and husband Glen as pastors.

L. Renee now serves as the WorldWide pastHER of Women of Vision and Destiny Ministries Worldwide, Inc. which celebrates 21 years of educating, empowering, and enlightening 1.6 million women worldwide. L. Renee leads a powHERful global teaching pastHERal team including Kim Miller, Jessy Augustine, Elaine Robison, Crystal

Wilhoite, and Beatrice Yesufu. WOVD also has a social media presence through WOVD TV on four continents (North America, Asia, Africa, and Australia), and audiences in India, Cameroon, China, Mexico, The Bahamas, Zambia, Papua New Guinea, United States, Nigeria, Malaysia, Taiwan, Philippines, Uganda, Pakistan, Canada, South Africa, Jamaica, Syria, Sierra Leone, and Kenya.

L. Renee and her pastHERal team are seen weekdays Monday-Friday on the Power Up Your Faith Show at www.facebook.com/WOVDWW/Live. Launched on in October 2017, the show airs at 6 a.m. central/7 a.m. eastern/4:30 India and has hosted more than 1,001 EPICsodes. WOVD Asia launched its Power UP Your Faith Show Asia in April 2021, and the WOVD 24/7 Prayer Chapel show launched in April 20/21. L. Renee is a social media powHERhouse and titan, and as a result of her adeptness and skill, the WOVD TV platform airs on 14Facebook pages and in ten Facebook groups. She can be found on LinkedIn, Instagram, and Twitter. The Vision 20/21 is to begin conversations with I-Heart and Sirus Radio to get these shows on global radio.

A credentialed intercessor by Living World Christian Center (Dr. Bill Winston), L. Renee loves to spend time with God. She walks through the Bible daily and has read the entire Bible over 20 times since 2000, a practice she learned from Dr. Horace E. Smith. She loves the Lord and spending time with Him in her prayer closet and during her mountain top prayer retreats. Her prayers have extended the lives of her husband, mother, and father who were afflicted by strokes, and thousands of others.

Known as the Billionaire Visionnaire, for 20 years L. Renee served as a media director, and the third highest-ranking woman of color, at the world's largest advertising and communications companies in Chicago. She managed $1 billion in advertising for Fortune 100 clients.

L. Renee and her husband, Glen, took a leap of faith and left the corporate world to live their big, bodacious, brilliant dream of business ownership. Together they opened a Marble Slab Creamery ice cream franchise on Michigan Avenue, which remained open for six years (2006-2012). The store served 1.2 million ice cream lovers across cultures and employed 100 young people, many of them inner-city youth, who learned the ropes of becoming leaders. The store was on the local and national news and visited by former Mayor Richard M. Daley of Chicago, local aldermen, celebrities, and loyal customers.

After the business closed in 2012 and her husband had a massive cerebral brain hemorrhage, L. Renee went through what she calls her pitch-black dark season and spent hours in her prayer closet, rebuilding her mind, body, and soul. In her prayer closet, she literally reinvented herself and reshaped her destiny. Inspired by a Bible story in 2 Kings 4 about the prophet Elijah and the widow heavily in debt, L. Renee designed her I AM Worth It story, discovered her own pot of olive oil, and turned it into an oil field.

L. Renee's journey is chronicled in her third book *The Widow Oil Tycoon: Ten Keys to Turn Your Pot of Oil into an Oil Field*, available on Kindle and Amazon. L. Renee travels around the world teaching the widow's story and empowering women in business, ministry, and corporate America at the Ultimate Women's Expo and other major events. Her Vision 20/21 focus is the Rich Gurlz Club Inc. and the Rich Gurlz Publish Books publishing company. This year L. Renee launched 40 Rich Gurlz Club authors in 90 days. She and her team are working on 50 book projects this year which will come out in Vision 20/21 and Vision 20/22. These books are now on Amazon, in Barnes and Noble, Target, Sears, Walgreens, and Walmart. The best way to reach her for speaking engagements is at www.wealthandrichestoday.com.

Chapter 2
Jacob's Mother Plots for the Blessing, A Mother's Send Off
(Genesis 27:1-17; 42-46)
L. Renee Richardson

The End of Life

Over the years, numerous doctors have told us that my mom had come to the end of her life. I have been hearing these prognoses since December 2018, when doctors convinced us to admit her to hospice care, which typically means there is a maximum of six months of life remaining. Today is August 23, 2021, I am in the Columbus, GA hospice with my mom as I write this chapter. We are here to give her essential fluids as she has stopped eating. We continue to exercise our faith fight because God has given us dominion and rulership over death.

The news of a loved one's impending departure can bring horror, shock, despair, and disbelief. That is, until we launch a faith fight. Just the thought of the one we love not being here is heart wrenching. The emotions, thoughts and feelings are overwhelming. In Genesis 27, we see the same thing happening when the Bible says, 'and it came to pass'. It's a part of life. As my mother's nurse, Tammy, shared with me yesterday, there is a miracle of birth and the miracle of death. I had never heard it explained that way before—the miracle of death. It sounds like a book to me; in fact, the nurses have given me books to read on the "end of life" process. They don't know I read these same books about a year ago when mom's health shifted. But last year, just as today, I have decided to fight the good fight of faith. I'm praying and asking God to let her rally again. I find those books hard to read as I am expecting long life for both of my parents, just as the Scriptures promise. God has answered my prayers over and over again. We have been through strokes, brain bleeds and life support machines. I have witnessed so many life extension miracles and am expecting one now! How? I am standing on the promise of John 11. Jesus said *I am* the Resurrection and the Life.

Ecclesiastes 3 proclaims, "To everything there is a season, and a time to every purpose under the heaven. A time to be born, and a time to die." And in the words that rolled off Moses' ink pen in Genesis, *it came to pass* that Issac was old. Old. It seems like only yesterday we witnessed Sarah laughing at thought of becoming pregnant and giving birth in her nineties to a child—the promised heir apparent, of Abraham—Isaac. Now we see that her only son's tour of duty on earth was coming to an end. He was going back to where he came from— eternity.

Issac Was Old

Issac was old. *Old.* I personally do not like the word old. I tell everyone I am 25. They laugh, but in my mind, I am 25 again. "So a man thinketh so is he," says Proverbs 23:7. I am blessed to have lived the abundant American Dream! The first 25 years of most of our lives are built by a kingdom of man's design. We can almost quote the American Dream instructions by heart. Quote it with me. Finish high school. Go to college. Get a college degree. Get a good job. Get married. Buy a house in the suburbs with a white picket fence. Have 2.5 children. Retire. Spend 40 years on the sofa watching re-runs of the top sitcoms from your youth. Think about the "shoulda, coulda, wouldas" of your life. Spend all those decades looking backward, but never forward. High school reunions become the rage because we do not know what to do with our "oldness."

Once I reached 25… again, I decided that I wanted more out of life. I began to think about what kind of life I wanted to live. In 2017, I wrote everything down in about fifteen "vision categories". We host a powerful event, I Have a Dream, on Dr. Martin Luther King Jr.'s birthday, empowering women on how to create the life they desire. Inspired in part by the women we serve, I dreamed big, bodacious, brilliant dreams. I learned kingdom principles that taught me how to create the life that I wanted. I began to live again, designing my own life, building my own massive dreams. I was blessed that after the bank closed the ice cream store my husband and I owned on Michigan Ave in Chicago in 2012, I set big goals for my life and set out on a journey. As I reflect on the toughest decade of my life, I can amazingly see the hand of God orchestrating His purpose and destiny for me. Here are the highlights.

In 2010, my "Chicago mom," Aunt Precious, had a stroke. In 2011, her husband, my Uncle Harold, had a stroke. In 2012 my 43-year-old husband had a massive cerebral hemorrhage. In 2018 my mom had a stroke. And in 2019, my father had a stroke and a brain bleed. Mom suffered a brain bleed later that year. In every one of these cases, God blessed us with miraculous healings.

Blind Fathers

Old. Genesis 27 reads like a best-selling book or a box office movie with its twists, turns, and divine salvations. Issac's eyes were so dim that he could not see. Moses does not reveal how Issac became blind. Did diabetes exist back then? All we know is that he could not see, and this lack of vision is going to impact the destinies of his sons. How many blind fathers do we have today? Ok, I will not go there. I believe the Bible patriarchs died a little differently than we do today. Hebrews 9:27 KJV says, "it is appointed unto men once to die." After Adam's fall in the Garden of Eden, we were all given an appointment with death. Sin booked the dates on our calendars. We all were appointed to die. I am personally working to schedule that appointment as late as possible and am designing how I want it to occur. I believe that I am fashioned by God to rule the world even over death.

At this time in our GODstory, Issac was old—did I say that already? He didn't know the specific day of his death, but he knew it was soon. He had unfinished business. He knew he had an assignment to leave his blessing for his eldest son, Esau. Esau had previously sold his birthright benefits to his younger brother Jacob but was still entitled to earn the blessing from his father.

The Father's Blessing: My Two Sons

Of his two sons Issac loved the oldest, Esau the outdoorsman, the most. As an old man, we can see Issac reminiscing about his younger days of hunting. I can relate as my grandparents have gifted us with land that my grandmother often let marksmen use for deer hunting. Being in the woods with nature is powerful. Issac told Esau to get his weapon, the quiver which held the arrows and bow for shooting, to kill some game and make him some venison. This is meat from a deer or edible game. He told his son to make him some savory meat that he loves to eat and bring it to him. He would then bless Esau from his soul and die. He had an appointment to keep.

I personally believe that the patriarchs booked their appointments with death. They saw it as a unique season and made provisions for it. What was Esau thinking about? Was it preparing his father's last meal, or was he so excited about the blessing that would mark the next phase of his life as the leader of the legendary family—Abraham, Issac, and Jacob. As it stood at that moment, his name was not to be written in the lineage of the "big three" of the Bible, instead Jacob's name would be included.

It seemed like an easy thing to do. Go hunting and prepare his father's last meal. These twin boys were born when Issac was sixty years old. Genesis 25:27-28 describes their differences and their parents' preferences for each child. "The boys grew up. Esau became an expert hunter, an outdoorsman. Jacob was a quiet man preferring life indoors amount the tents. Issac loved Esau because he loved the game, but Rebekah loved Jacob." Esau had hunted his entire life. He loved the joy he would see on his father's face when he would bring in his rewards from hunting! There was nothing like it. In the world of hunting, Esau was a natural winner, easily triumphing his twin brother. Esau was a winner. He often compared himself to his twin brother who was a momma's boy. Jacob was a plain man, a tent dweller. They were twins, yet so different. We saw them fight in the womb, and that battle was still going on. Esau was terribly sorry that he had sold his birthright to his younger brother, but today was different. Esau believed he was going to be named the winner, the undefeated champion. The winner of the elusive father's blessing. Now he was off to the woods to gather his father's venison.

A Mother's Plan to Win

The only challenge was that his mother Rebekah was eavesdropping on Issac and Esau's conversation. She knew the days of her husband were numbered as each day he became weaker and weaker. Was she listening for the date when Issac would confer the blessing? As she washed the dishes over the last few months and Issac's health declined, she must have known this day would come. Her only concern was that she wanted the father's blessing to go to her favorite son, Jacob. As she washed the dishes and prepared meals, I believe she began to devise a SHE-strategy to ensure her favorite twin would get the father's blessing. She was ear hustling to learn when this transfer was going to take place.

A Mother's Scheme
"Now therefore, my son, obey my voice according to that which I command thee."
—Genesis 27:8

It sounds like she had planned it. Meditated on it. Her favorite twin boy was going to get what she felt was due to him. Do what I tell you to do, Jacob. He was a momma's boy. He liked the kitchen. His culinary gifts allowed him to secure the birthright from Esau. Now the only thing left was the father's blessing. Jacob was reluctant about the plan. He knew that his skin was smooth, Esau's skin was hairy. How could his mom make it work? Jacob feared the trickery would result in his dad cursing him. To be cursed would be much worse than not receiving the blessing. Rebekah had meditated on how to "steal" or trick Esau out of the father's blessing. Deception ran in the family. We often think it came from the father's side, but I believe it came from Rebekah's. Her brother Laban, Jacob and Esau's uncle, was a seasoned trickster.

Rebekah Prepares the Hearty Meal
Rebekah cooked the hearty meal that she knew her husband loved so much. Then she took the dress-up clothes of her older son Esau and put them on her younger son Jacob. She took goatskins and covered his hands and the smooth nape of his neck. Then she placed the hearty meal she had fixed and fresh bread she'd baked into the hands of her son. She had thought of everything that would be needed to convince blind Isaac that Jacob was his older twin brother.

Jacob is declared lord!
Rebekah's plot worked! Jacob received the blessing. Jacob won! He was declared lord over his brother. It was official. It was irreversible. He won the corn and wine blessing. Then Esau came in from hunting and found that his blessing had been given to Jacob.   Furious, he

said, "The time for mourning my father's death is close. And then I'll kill my brother Jacob" Genesis 27:41 TM. When these words were rehearsed to Rebekah, she had to create another plot, this time to send her favorite son off. Jacob received the father's blessing but lost his family.

A Mother's Send Off
Now Rebekah had to send her favorite child to her brother Laban. Her strategy was that Jacob would live with Laban until Esau cooled down and his anger subsided, and he forgot what Jacob did to him. Her plan was to send for him to come back later. I believe her words were, "Why should I lose both of you on the same day?"

Rebekah was experiencing the pain of Eve, the world's first mother. In her situation, two brothers competed for their father's love and in the end, Cain killed his brother Abel. The Bible continues to repeat itself. We talk about Eve's pain in experiencing the loss of the child in our book, *Fashioned by God to Rule the World*. I remember hearing a story about a mom whose son killed his brother in their home. Rather than lose both sons, the family placed the dead son's body in the car and told the police that the killer was walking the streets. Like Rebekah, this mom sent her other son away to protect him from the law. And like Rebekah, she did not want to lose both sons in one day.

While Jacob received the father's blessing, he lost his family in the process. What price are you willing to pay for things that are designed for others? Jacob coveted Esau's firstborn position even before they were born. In the first chapter of this book, by Flossie Berry, we see the battle between brothers started in the womb. In the Bible, the womb struggle was so intense that Rebekah desired to die during her pregnancy. She sought the Lord to find out what was going on. In Genesis 25:21-23, the Lord told her that the womb war was bigger than carrying twins. She was carrying nations. Wow. This was a glimpse of destiny. Where we see babies, God sees nations. What nation are you carrying in your womb?

At their birth, the twins were fighting for the number one

position. Esau won the oldest position by birth, but Jacob was clutching tight to Esau's heel at the time of delivery. Jacob's name meant "heel". At their birth, their destinies collided. Despite his firstborn position, the older brother was destined to serve the younger. But to God, it was not about age. It was about destiny. Jacob lost the battle in the womb, but he spent the rest of his life chasing that first born position. What have you been seeking since your childhood for which you are willing to trick and steal? Rebekah desired Jacob, the younger child, to be the firstborn, too. She spent her life seeking ways for him to be elevated in the eyes of their father. But in the end, she never knew how things turned out for her sons. The Bible does not record Rebekah's death and we have no idea if she ever saw her favorite son again.

Chapter 3

A Mother and Father's Instructions for Wife Selection
(Genesis 27:46; Genesis 28:1-2, 5-9)
Dr. Janet Benson, RN, BSN, MS, M.Ed, Ed.D PEL-CSN

Janet's HERstory

Dr. Janet James-Benson is first and foremost a Christian. Her relationship with Christ provides the guidance, motivation and strength she has needed, her entire life. Janet was born, literally at home, and raised on the south side of Chicago. Her mother shared the story of her birth. She was born at 6:30 in the morning, and totally unexpected, as she was two months premature!

Her mom described the way Janet's dad called the fire department and then ran to the elevator, taking it down to the first floor of their apartment building and stopped anyone from using it until the fire personnel arrived. Janet was taken to the Newberry Health Center where she was assessed and cared for by Nurse Midwives. Before she was taken away, her older sister gave her a nickname. While her sister was walking around looking at all the excitement, she pointed to Janet and said "Be Be?" instead of baby. It is still her nickname sixty-four years later.

Janet was enrolled in the Chicago Public School system from kindergarten through high school. After high school, Janet attended DePaul University where she received a Bachelor of Science in Nursing and she began her health care career as a Registered Nurse. She continued to enhance her education. In 2003, she received a Master of Science in Health Services Administration from the University of St. Francis. In 2012, a Master of Education from the American College of Education and in December of 2020 a Doctorate in Educational Leadership, also from the American College of Education.

Janet began her nursing practice at Rush Medical Center and was employed there for a total of 25 years. She has been employed as a School Nurse with Chicago Public Schools since 1999 and at one point she worked at both Rush and CPS. Janet loves caring for and educating God's people. She is very active in her church; she sings in the choir and serves on the church's health ministry.

Janet enjoys being a wife of 23 years to Sidney Benson Sr., mother to Jonathan and Sidney Jr. and grandmother to Noah Lopez. She enjoys her daughter-in-love, Dominique, and her cousin Michelle Smith whom she has mothered for the past 40 plus years. When not working, singing in the choir, or serving on the health ministry at her church, she can be found reading, playing chess, journaling or mentoring several young women she calls her "daughters".

Janet's desire to contribute to this manuscript is born out of her joy in helping others. It is her hope that this story will help both men and women understand that the only true, unfailing love comes from God. This doesn't mean our relationships are not valuable, important, or based on love and trust. However, the goal of this book is to emphasize that the only everlasting love is found in Christ Jesus.

Chapter 3
A Mother and Father's Instructions for Wife Selection
(Genesis 27:46; Genesis 28:1-2, 5-9)
Dr. Janet Benson

Have you always obeyed your parents? When you did, were you rewarded with what you expected and desired? When you disobeyed, did you find yourself in trouble, or at the very least, disappointed? Sometimes we do not always listen to our parents or our elders. We go our own way, making decisions we think are best. Many times, we think we know what is best for us. Unfortunately, we often find our best-laid plans can lead to disappointment, pain, and at times, a broken heart.

When we read the chapters in Genesis which outline the relationships between Jacob, Esau, their parents, Rebekah and Isaac, and Leah and Rachel, we see deception, dishonesty, selfishness, trickery, heartbreak, and disobedience. The deception and dishonesty first appear when Rebekah, Esau and Jacob's mother, convinces Jacob to deceive his father, Isaac, (Genesis 27:28-29), resulting in Jacob getting the blessing which was intended for the firstborn, Esau. This deception caused division within the family, hurt feelings, anger and a broken heart. Rebekah's displeasure with Esau's choice of wives, Hittite (or Canaanite) women, caused Rebekah to take matters into her own hands and make sure her favorite son, Jacob, received a blessing he did not earn.

Although it is not clear exactly why Isaac and Rebekah disapproved of Esau's choices, we know that there was to be no intermarrying between Abraham's decedents and the inhabitants of Canaan. Nevertheless, Esau made the decision to disobey his parents and the Bible tells us, this caused his mother much grief. The Canaanites and Hittites were people who were known for their evil culture. The laws of the day protected the Hittite women. They could initiate a divorce and had the legal right to keep the inheritance and their half of the husband's estate. I think it's safe to say, most mothers who genuinely love and care for our sons, would not want them to marry a woman whom we consider to be unworthy.

My first marriage, which ended in a divorce, was not something my dad was happy about. He was not happy about the marriage but the divorce that was another story. However, when it ended, he was gracious enough not to say, "I told you so". In fact, he provided me the love and support I needed to get through what was a painful, humiliating, and embarrassing experience. That experience was one of the most devastating episodes of my life, and it left me feeling unloved.

How often have we been willing to be deceptive, dishonest, and disobedient to gain instant gratification, only to find that what we have done brings us pain in the long run. Even though we may initially feel good about our successful manipulation, when we step outside of the will of God, we ultimately feel unsatisfied and disappointed. Throughout Genesis chapter 25 through 27 we are shown that when we step ahead of God, and end up hurt, His love, grace and mercy continue to cover us. As we see in this chapter, Jacob receives the blessings from his father, and becomes a great man as God promised his grandfather, Abraham.

What causes us to feel unloved? Is it that we do not receive the time, attention, and affection we believe we deserve? Perhaps when we do receive those things, we realize they are not what we wanted, or they weren't presented in the way we had hoped. Have you ever been looking forward to an upcoming event that you've planned and shopped for? Perhaps you've hired an event planner to help, and you spend months making sure everything is perfect. You select the right colors, the right food, the right decorations, the right guests and of course, the right outfit. After spending an enormous amount of time preparing, the day finally comes. And in a matter of a few hours, it's over. How do you feel? Are you a little let down? Did your guests not compliment you the way you thought they would? Did your loved ones not tell you how terrific you are and what a great job of planning you did? Did your significant other forget to tell you how amazing you are and that your planning skills are impeccable?

Even if we do receive accolades and praises, we can still feel let down. This is especially true when we look to external resources to make us feel good. Motivational writer, William Arthur Ward, wrote something that I saw more than 25 years ago, and it still rings true to me today, "Happiness is an inside job. Don't assign anyone else that much power over your life". Isn't it amazing how we do that? As women we sometimes look to our family, best friends or a significant other to make us feel affirmed, wanted, needed. When we start to think that our close circle of friends, family or loved ones are not giving us what we think they should, we can become angry, bitter, and resentful. In reality, it is not their job to satisfy all of our needs or make us feel loved. I have had to come to the realization that although my husband compliments my life, he is not responsible for making me happy. That's between me and God.

During the times in my marriage when I don't feel loved, I have learned to stop and ask myself and God, "where should my focus be?" It never fails. God's response is always, "On Me!" I can always tell when I have moved away from my relationship with God, which is truly the only relationship where true happiness can consistently be found. I can tell by looking at my environment. Is my house cluttered? Do I have too much stuff on my work desk, preventing me from finding what I need? Am I irritable and snapping at my husband, or are my responses dripping with sarcasm? Usually, when I can answer "yes" to three of these questions, I know I have drawn away from God.

I don't mean that I am in a backslidden state. I mean I have stopped praying in the morning before I start my day. I have stopped reading my scriptures and spending quiet, meditative time with the Lord. I have not asked Him what He would have me do today. I can honestly say, those are the times I feel the lowest in my spirit, and unloved. John 13:34 tells us that God's love is giving and unselfish. When I read that scripture, I am reminded, that perhaps I need to come out of my feelings and consider the feelings of others. Do something for someone else, just because.

I compare feeling unloved to a heart attack. When a person has a heart attack, it is usually caused by a combination of things, a blocked blood vessel, damage to the heart muscle, tightening or constriction of the blood vessel, or perhaps an abnormal heart rhythm. There are many things that can lead to a heart attack, but in general, the result is something dies. Even though the person who has the attack may survive it, a part of their heart muscle will die. That part of the muscle will never rejuvenate itself. It is gone forever. But, because we are "fearfully and wonderfully made," and we have access to state-of-the-art health care, we can be placed on medication, improve our nutrition and lifestyle and we can continue to live. But we must not forget, the heart has to heal. The heart has been damaged. For many people who feel unloved, the heart has most likely been damaged.

Sometimes our heart attack or heart damage can start in our early childhood. Maybe we did not grow up in a home with both parents present. Maybe both were present, but there were rarely demonstrations of love and affection between the two. Perhaps our parents did not show love and affection to us. Maybe we didn't get the hug and the "I love you" or the "You did a great job" from mom or dad, that we desired. Perhaps we spent our lives in the care of aunts, uncles, grandparents, foster parents, older siblings or adoptive parents. Maybe we were the victim of some unspeakable physical, sexual, emotional or mental trauma from which we have not healed. Somewhere along the line the damage may have occurred.

We moved on. We became adults. We began to have relationships with others. We looked for love. We needed love. The need for love is a normal, human emotion. Most psychological literature speaks to how important that need is. There are studies that talk about an infant's need to be held and swaddled in order to grow. As a nurse, I have cared for patients recovering in the hospital after a major surgical procedure. Patients who had family and friends calling or coming to visit, had shorter hospital stays and quicker recoveries. Those who were alone or had no visitors, tended to recover slower, had more complications, and stayed hospitalized longer.

The Scriptures also show us what God thought about aloneness. When He looked at all He had made He said, "it is good". When He looked at Adam, alone in the garden, that was the only time God said, something was not good. This for me is an awesome revelation, because God made everything! So how could there be something "not good". I believe God wanted us to see that being alone, and isolated was not His plan for us and "it is not good". He created Eve, who was a suitable companion for Adam. Even though the Bible does not tell us a lot about Adam's initial reaction when he met Eve, it tells us enough to know that Adam was happy and loved.

So, what do we see in Chapters 27 and 28 of Genesis? We see a mother completely dissatisfied with her oldest son's choice of wife. Here is a mother ensuring that her favorite son, Jacob, gets the inheritance due his unloved older brother, Esau. Then there is Esau, disobeying his parents' direction, and marrying the wrong woman. Esau is willing to give up his birthright for a plate of food, not considering the long-term consequences of his actions. We see aspects of ourselves in these scriptures—the bitterness and anger that comes from realizing we have made a mistake and how this can make us resentful. This chapter reminds us that instant gratification can lead to bad decisions and missed blessings. For some of us, our bad decisions lead to undesired results for which we choose to blame others. It is at these times that we often are reminded to turn back to God. Only He can heal us and bring us out of these unwieldy and destructive situations.

In Chapter 27 we also see Jacob's mom conjuring up a scheme to ensure that the blessing is given to her favorite son. Not only is she being deceptive to her older son, but she is fooling her husband. As a result of her own deception and trickery, she is forced to send her favorite son away for his safety. The scriptures tell us that Jacob's parents instruct him not to marry a Canaanite woman, which is another reason he was sent away. Once Esau realizes how displeased his parents are with his choice of wife, he goes to his uncle Ismael and marries one of his daughters, who is actually, Esau's half-cousin! The scriptures imply that Esau believed if he married someone in the family, she would be an acceptable choice in the eyes of his parents.

There are many lessons to be learned in these two Bible chapters. Most of life's lessons start with us becoming introspective and meditative. We cannot understand our motivations and actions without having a connection with our Creator. How often have we done something we know is wrong or unwise and later ask "why did I do that?" God has blessed us with the gift of free will. I came to really understand this when I began to study the beginning of the Bible. I asked, "If God knew Adam and Eve were going to eat from the forbidden tree, why did He put it there in the first place?" As I continued to study His Word, I understood. He doesn't want to drag us by our hair into submission. He wants us to come to Him of our own accord because He loves us and wants a relationship with us.

When we hear the voice of God, whether through His Word, another person, a song or a minister, we need to receive it and obey. The will of God blesses us. He tells us repeatedly and shows us throughout the Bible the benefits of obedience. He made us, He knows us, and He loves us. When we strike out on our own, doing what we want to do, grasping for what we think will make us happy, we tend to lose. Sure, there are times when we get what we want and we enjoy it. But when what we obtain is outside the will of God, can we honestly say it was fulfilling? Often we are left feeling a sense of emptiness, loneliness, and incompleteness. The new car, the new job, the raise in pay, the new relationship are all good things and for most of us, it took hard work and dedication to make those achievements. I believe God wants us to have all of that, but not without Him.

When the issues of life cause us to sin, which is anything that takes us away from time with God, we suffer. Doing things God's way makes life fulfilling and productive. It does not mean we will be without challenges and devastating events that cause us pain, but what it does mean is that God will never leave us alone. We do not have to help God in His plan for our lives. His promises can be enjoyed, and we can prosper when we obey Him. Our relationship with Him can be restored through obedience. We can find real peace and true love, in our relationship with Him. Throughout many chapters of the Bible we see where God's people decided to move ahead of God's timing. We see it with Abraham and Sarah. We see it again with Leah and Rachel, both working to please their husband Jacob. It is amazing how far we will go to secure the love of others, but when they don't our hearts are broken. We suffer a type of heart attack and something in us dies.

Genesis 27 and 28, show us that we all have character flaws and defects. But God can still use us if we turn from our ways and seek His.

God made a promise to Abraham, who was the grandfather to Jacob and Esau, and He kept that promise. He prospered Jacob because of his willingness to repent and turn back to God. Each generation, from Abraham down, had character flaws and deficiencies, but that did not stop God from using them to accomplish His will on earth. I believe this is one of the greatest Bible lessons for us to learn.

No matter what we have done or how long we have done it, God's love is available. Unfortunately for many of us, we look for that kind of unconditional love to come from mankind. No human being is capable of loving us the way God does. Even as parents, we love our children and for some of us would even die for them, but we are imperfect creations. We are not capable of truly unselfish, unconditional love. We try but we cannot come close to demonstrating the love God has for us. We do ourselves and our relationships a disservice when we expect that our partner will meet every need and satisfy ever longing. God's love is pure, consistent, uplifting, powerful and satisfying. When we develop an authentic relationship with God, He allows us to see our shortcomings. Unlike Esau who became so angry with Jacob that he wanted to kill him, God's love will allow us to take a look at the part we played in the unwanted circumstances we find ourselves in. Even when we experience pain at the hands of others over which we had no control, God tells us that He is still bigger than our circumstances, and if we are faithful to Him, He will be faithful to comfort us through whatever concerns us.

In these chapters, Genesis 27 and 28, there are hard lessons. Obedience to our parents, those in authority over us, our church leaders, and most of all to God, yields desired results even when we cannot see them. Abraham's wife gave her maidservant to her husband, showing her lack of faith in God's promise that she would bear him a child. God still blessed Abraham and Sarah. Isaac mistakenly gave his youngest son the blessing owed to his oldest son, and Jacob tricked his father, but God still kept His promise and blessed Jacob. Both these men turned their hearts to God, and He increased their faith. The same gift is offered to us.

The Bible shows us Jacob in being transformed in this chapter.

According to the Life Application Study Bible, Jacob's name, means "grasps the heel", which he did in his mother's womb. He literally grabbed his brother's heel as they were being born. He later grabbed his brother's birthright and blessing. When Jacob fled from his home and the wrath of his brother, he had an encounter with God through an angel, with whom he grabbed a hold of. It was at that point that Jacob became aware of his dependence on God and how God had kept His promises, His covenant, and continued to bless Jacob. In the final stage of his transformation, God grabbed Jacob and in so doing, He changed his name to Israel which literally means "he struggles with God". Jacob became the father of the twelve tribes of Israel. What a blessing!

The Bible proves to us that obedience to God brings life-sustaining blessings and contentment. It does not mean we will be pain-, trouble- or tribulation-free. It does mean that we have a Father who loves us and cares about us. He knows what we have need of, and He knows about the desires of our hearts. He knows the roads we have traveled and the ones yet to come. The only way to enjoy the benefits of God's promises is to obey Him. Disobedience to God is sin. Sin brings about death—death of a relationship, death of our joy, peace, and contentment and possibly death to our bodies, just like the heart attack. Obedience, faith, submission, humility and commitment to God is what is required for real love. God will never disappoint, trick, deceive or abandon us. Daily, He shows us what real love is. Once we establish an authentic relationship with Him, we never have to feel unloved again. God bless you all.

Chapter 4

A Mother and Father's Instructions for Wife Selection
(Genesis 27:46; Genesis 28:1-2, 5-9)
Dr. Crystal Neumann, DBA, MAED, MBA, BBA, BS, MH, CHT, RYT 200

Crystal's HERstory

Dr. Crystal Neumann is an educator in higher education, a spiritual worker, a lifelong learner, and proponent of the "body, mind, spirit" philosophy. She balances her academic side, in which she has a doctoral degree in business administration, with the imaginative and inventive part of her being. She is an accomplished speaker, who has a passion for sharing new findings with others. She has offered lectures and workshops nationally and internationally on varying topics from faculty and curriculum development, to mindfulness, and herbalism. Dr. Neumann is also a published researcher; she is constantly curious and wanting to find all the answers. Some research topics include leadership, sustainability, and critical thinking.

With an eccentric nature, she has pursued creative and inspirational writing. Dr. Neumann believes powerful stories can change the world, transporting readers to a place where women are the courageous heroines, fantasy can be visualized into reality, and character flaws are endearing. She also loves expression emotions through haikus and other forms of poetry. To her friends and family, Crystal is notorious for her quirky personality, captivating storytelling abilities, and expressive imagination through words, pressed flower art, and guided meditations. When she's not writing, she can be found partaking in one of her many eclectic hobbies. She might be getting her hands dirty in the garden, teaching yoga, throwing knives, or cosplaying with her terribly uncoordinated lightsaber skills.

Outside of her accomplishments and hobbies, she is a daughter, sister, aunt, wife, mother, and friend among many other roles. She was born and raised in a Hispanic neighborhood on the southside of Chicago. As a first generation American, she understands the responsibility she has in being a voice to support equity, diversity, and inclusion. She always strives to be a role model for others, which is why she takes great pride in being a mentor, dissertation chair, and teacher.

Chapter 4
Capturing a Man's Heart: A Woman's Kiss that Makes a Man Cry
(Genesis 29:1-13)
Dr. Crystal Neumann

Jacob continued his journey in the direction which the sun rises, in the east. He made his way toward his relative's home, Laban. Nearing his destination, Jacob arrived upon a scene in which there were a few men and a watering well, out in the middle of the field. There were three flocks of sheep laying around the well, just waiting. It was still warm out, and the sheep looked thirsty and tired, much like everyone else. It did not appear as though the flocks were able to get a sip of water just yet. There was a large stone covering the well of refreshment.

Jacob drew closer and approached the shepherds, making a little bit of small talk. After all, it was quite the trip to get there. Much time was spent alone with his own thoughts, perhaps a little too much time for reflection. Loneliness gets kind of old after a while, in which human interaction was desperately needed. Therefore, a little companionship was completely welcomed. Jacob asked where the shepherds were from, whether they knew Laban, and if Laban was doing well. Jacob felt more relaxed and welcomed as the conversation continued. As they all chitchatted, one of the shepherds casually interrupted the discussion, noting that Rachel, Laban's daughter, was arriving with her flock.

As Jacob turned to look at the direction where the shepherd was pointing out, time stopped for the traveler. Jacob's gaze was fixated upon this soft feminine figure moving gracefully through the field. It was like she floated directly from the heavens. Her flock followed her, making Rachel look like a heroine— a leading lady with her loyal companions. The way the breeze brushed through her hair and clothing, she simply looked majestic.

Jacob's jaw dropped in awe at the sight of her. All he could do was take in her presence. Nothing around him mattered. All speech or sounds around him became muted. He heard nothing else. He only saw her. She became his sole focus. The scene around her faded into the background. He was completely speechless.

* * *

Jacob's Point of View

When I saw her, I was breathless. The wind was knocked out of me. The sun beamed upon her and she radiated such indescribable beauty. It was like nothing around me mattered anymore. Everyone disappeared, and Rachel was all I could see. It was as if she and I were the only ones who existed on earth. Time stopped. Yet, within a blink of an eye, I could see an incredible future. I could see several scenes of what was to come—all of the possibilities that were in store for me, for her, for us. I could see she and I wrapped in each other's arms for all eternity. I could see her becoming my wife, my best friend, confidant, and the mother of my children. I could see us laughing together, celebrating milestones, sharing a lifetime of joy. Thinking about our future together made me feel a surge of power throughout my body.

We may disagree, argue, or even bicker. But at the end of the day, we would love each other. I would make it my life's purpose to make her laugh and be the reason for her happiness. A smile from her beautiful face would make me fall in love with her every single time, just as I am feeling in this very moment. I would be blessed to be able to call myself her husband one day.

I don't think I ever believed in something like love at first sight. As I reflect on the concept further, I really can't say that I have. I never believed that anyone could ever look at someone and think that they could fall in love so quickly. How foolish and cynical I've been my entire existence! Yet, as my eyes search through her eyes —the window to her heart, I want to know her. I want to discover her likes, dislikes, and explore every story she has to share. She has my heart. It is so hard to explain, but I just love her. I suppose when you know, you *really* know. I've heard of such things happening to other people, and I would laugh at them because it sounded all so ridiculous. I wholeheartedly never thought this would happen to me either. Now that it has, I just want her to love me back.

Her eyes are sweet poetry. I could explore her eyes for the meaning of life and know that my purpose is to be right there in front of her, love her, and give her the world with everything I have. Her locks of hair flow softly like butterflies drifting in the wind. She has a smile as bright as the fullest moon, like a guiding light in the darkness. I could imagine all the sweet words that would escape from her lush lips. She should breathe life into me. I looked at her hands. They are small and delicate—hands I would love to hold and protect. Her command and presence demand the attention of her flock, just as she captures my thoughts and conquers my heart.

I yearn to learn more about her, her thoughts, and mind. Yet, I fear with all this love, she may not feel the same. Is it possible for love at first sight to be only one-sided? When I think about my love and this fear that has just come over me, the only metaphor that seems to escape my mind is that she is the sun, and I am the moon. What if we never fully embrace each other? Would we not collide? I would be obliterated by her warmth and heat like that of the sun, but at the same time, she is what completes me. She shines, and I can see clearly because of her. If I think about her absence in my life, my days would just be comprised of endless gloom. My biggest fear is that I cannot prevail without her. Instead of existing in separate spaces like the sun and the moon, I want us to exist as waves crashing into the sand with her – intertwined and never one without the other.

I am burdened by self-doubt, and my heart drops. My stomach churns. I feel empty and worthless. For a moment, my legs become wobbly, as they can no longer support my weight. The world around me spins around my head for several seconds. It's harder to breathe and my mouth feels like sandpaper. I can see the faces of my family and their disappointed looks, which I've seen several times before in my life.

What if she wants someone more like Esau? Some might say he's more handsome than I am. He's everything I'm not – strong, burly, hairy, rough and someone who catches game with brute force. I am a man who enjoys listening and good conversation. I love spending time with my mother and outside in nature. I enjoy good food. I am more of a thinker, and I think myself quick- witted. My mind is strong, but my arms are not. I could never live up to what my father wanted me to be, more like my brother. What if I disappoint her the way I have disappointed my father?

I am also not a man with riches. I have nothing to my name, and my pockets are completely empty. I don't have much, but I can give her all of my heart. I can do everything in my power to make her happy. I can at least try. I hope this love is returned. I would not wish unrequited love on anyone because the thought alone is unbearable.

I pray Rachel would live in bliss with someone like me. I need to demonstrate to her I *can* be someone who has courage and strength – someone who also demands attention just in the exact same way she does. I have to show her I *am* worthy of her love. I can be the one she settles down with.

"Jacob and Rachel," I love the sound of that. I know with certainty and every cell in my being that she is the love of my life. I shall always remind her with every moment that we would share, how in love I am with her – that she is the sweetest, most beautiful woman I have ever laid eyes on. I can show her that she is my life's treasure. There is only one way for me to find out how she feels. It is my hope that with everything that has happened, and everything that I have been through, that God will reward me.

Rachel's Point of View

There was nothing remarkable about the day. It's the same chores, but just on a different day in this boring town. I yearn for something different each morning that I wake up. My father doesn't care about me, or anyone else. He doesn't care about anyone unless there is something that can be gained from that person. I am merely a possession in his eyes, someone who takes up space, or an extra mouth to feed. I exist, which is very different from living. I pray to God that something spectacular can happen so I can just find my way out of this place.

More than just getting out of my father's house, I hope to have some excitement in my life. I could find myself an adventure, see more of the world, and even meet the love of my life. Everyone wants to find love, and I'm no different. What does it feel like to have your heart pitter- patter for someone? I want to feel that too. I want to fall *madly* in love. I want to find someone who is attentive and understanding. This man should also make me laugh. Yes, I want to have good belly laughs and have fun with my sweetheart.

I just want to find my other half. I see couples together, and when they are in love, they all have that same doe-eyed look in each other's eyes. I want someone to look at me with the same adoration.

When these couples laugh, it's like they have lost all common sense. They are on their own planet together, giggling on about things no one else understands or finds humorous. I wish to lose my own senses with the man of my dreams.

While I have all these hopes and dreams, I must go on and exist until something wondrous occurs so that I can finally *live*. I have faith my time will come. I have prayed and prayed. I must simply be patient and wait for my turn.

I took my flock to their usual watering hole. There seemed to be someone new there amongst my friends. This was someone I don't think I've ever seen before. I don't immediately recognize him. His back was turned to me. It was angular and strong. As I get closer, one of the shepherds pointed me out to the stranger. When he turned around, I was captivated. My heart skipped a beat.

I looked up and I saw this man. I saw this *handsome* man. His skin was flawless. It was as if my fingertips could glide across the smoothest silk. His stature was not overbearing, but he was lean. I could tell he was a different kind of man, more sensitive – someone who could cater to my emotions, feel with me, talk about profound topics with me, and intellectually stimulate me. He had the kind eyes of a caring and deep, thoughtful soul. He looked at me with such admiration. His demeanor completely changed in an instant from looking tired and unimpressed to mesmerized. His eyes lit up and his smile was dashing. In this moment, all I could do was shyly flash a smile back. I could tell he was a charmer.

I've never had anyone capture my attention like this before. There is something different about him and the way he looked into my eyes from a distance. It's like we have known each other's hearts and spirits for lifetimes.

Yet, there appeared to be a fleeting moment of uncertainty, doubt, and even sadness. His face went from bright sunshine rays invading the earth's atmosphere to falling like aimless, withered leaves from an autumn tree. His face expressed serious loss. This is usually the face I would see from someone who lost all hope. Oh no, what have I done? But I haven't done anything yet. Does he not like me anymore? I didn't say anything. Should I have said something? Was he just being kind and nice, like his eyes tell me he is?

He turned to talk to the shepherds. I don't know what they all said exactly, but I'm left in a state of confusion. I search for an answer within his eyes, but he's no longer looking at me. I could no longer read his face. Once again, he's a stranger to me. Perhaps today isn't the day I thought it would be. I suppose today is not the day I would experience the excitement and love I've been praying for. I should not have gotten my hopes up.

My eyes still followed his movement out of curiosity. I would be lying if I said there wasn't still some sliver of hope that he could be the one for me. It seemed that he was done talking to the group. The man moved with motivation toward the watering well. His eyes stared intently at the stone over the well. He examined it with such scrutiny, like he was about to conquer some kind of mission. I know from watching other shepherds before, there were usually a few men helping each other out to move the stone. I wondered who he would ask for help.

However, this man who literally walked into my life, used all his strength and might to remove the stone *by himself*. He moved the stone as if this was some heroic effort to offer water to the sheep. The stone was all there was that was standing between a dry parched mouth and fulfillment of thirst. Never in my life have I ever seen just one man remove that stone with this level of purpose and willpower. His grit was quite attractive. My goodness, I think he was trying to impress me! After the flocks drank this water, they could go back to rest and bask in the sun, feeling more refreshed.

The attractive man made his way towards me. This time he looked even more determined. As he walked closer to me, I felt my own heart pounding in my chest – faster and faster. He must have felt the same, as his breathing has quickened the pace. I saw his chest puffing up and down with every breath he took. When I looked at his eyes, his pupils dilated. My own eyes may have deceived me, but I could almost see a bead of sweat upon his forehead. We were like two magnets drawn to each other. It feels as though God made him just for me, and I just for

70

him. Finally, once and for all, I can leave this place and live my life. All my hopes, dreams, and prayers have led me to this very moment, *my* moment!

He grabbed my face and stared into my eyes for only a few seconds, though those few seconds felt like an eternity. He studied my face as if to memorize the path towards his destiny. Yes, please Lord, let me be his destiny. Then within an instant, he kissed me with such sweet and pure passion. It was as if he was a starved man for love. So I gave everything I could down to the very last breath that I could give, every droplet of my love. If he was starved for love, how could I not offer him a feast?

When I could no longer breathe, I broke away to gaze back into his eyes. To my surprise, he was weeping. Was this out of relief? Happiness? Both? All I could do in this moment was smile at him, reassuring him that true never ending love has been discovered at last. Neither of us would ever yearn to search for the other again. He has found me. God has led him to me to bless both of us. We could begin a wonderful future together.

* * *

It was obvious for any onlooker to take notice of the remarkable scene that just unfolded between the two new lovers. Jacob and Rachel were both breathless holding each other, both insanely blushing various shades of red. Jacob looked at Rachel with his beautiful face, boyish smile, and his warm heart. His smile went from ear to ear. He was feeling as though all of the hard times were over. He was finally going to get to experience true happiness, without feeling like he wasn't good enough, without feeling like he would never fulfill some unobtainable expectation of who he was supposed to be. Jacob fully intended on asking for her hand in marriage. He knew she was meant to be his future bride.

Rachel smiled back with glee and excitement. Her sweet face was beaming. She felt she was going to venture out toward something more exciting where she could feel alive. This was the start of something special and spectacular for her. This could be the first day of the rest of her life. It was in that moment, she knew, whenever Jacob decided to get down on one knee, be it today, tomorrow, or ten years

71

from now, to ask her to marry him, it would be yes – a thousand times, yes.

There was such a sweet look of fondness they held as they gazed into each other's eyes. The moment was perfect. Love was in the air. One could only hope that whatever they were feeling, it could be infectious. Jacob was in love with Rachel, and Rachel loved him back. This was a moment to cherish and remember.

Author's Story

Love at first sight hits people in different ways and at different points in life. In sophomore year of high school, I had a pen pal from Germany. His sister happened to be staying in the Chicago area for student exchange. I met his sister and parents when they needed a tour guide for downtown Chicago. I never met this boy—I had only seen in a few photographs, but we were open, honest, and authentic to each other in our letters, emails, and expensive long-distance phone calls. This was before today's webcams and smartphones. For years, we exchanged foreign candy, funny stories, and hardships.

I finally went to meet him face-to-face in Germany, six years after our first correspondence. On the flight there, I worried about whether this guy would like me. I worried that the spark I thought we had shared was only a figment of my imagination—that it was all in my head. I fought with my thoughts on how I might have been that hopeless romantic who was in love with the thought of being in love. Was I *that* girl who saw something that was never really there? I also didn't have anything to offer. I was a penniless 22-year-old, who'd already experienced a failed marriage, but had the most perfect little three-year-old boy.

When I got off my flight to visit him for the very first time, I saw him waiting for me from a distance. I was so excited. My stomach was in knots. My heart fluttered. My body was shaking with the built-up excitement. I was drawn to him like a moth to a flame. I didn't want to run toward him for fear that he would be disappointed. Maybe I sounded prettier over the phone or in the photos than I ever could be in person. I would have made a fool out of myself to run up to him only for a friendly handshake. I was so distracted I didn't pay attention to where I was going and set off an airport alarm for going in the wrong direction. What an embarrassing first impression!

However, the alarm did momentarily snap me out of being nervous to the point that I could really look at this gorgeous man's face. He was even more handsome in person. He had the cheesiest grin. It was a grin of anticipation, like a child waiting to open their first present on Christmas morning. He had a backpack on and fumbled with the backpack straps, as if he was trying to redirect his own nervous energy elsewhere. He smelled of fresh cologne and mint, as if he was getting ready for a first date himself. It was then I knew he was just as excited as I was. This was the day I met my husband in person.

Little did we know, his sister and best friend were observing us from another part of the airport. They took a picture of our first encounter. It was clear that we were already in love.

Chapter 5

A Tale of Two Sisters: Leah and Rachel
(Genesis 29:16-30)
Dr. Sheriolyn Curry – aka "Dr. Joy," BS, MDiv, CSA

Dr. Joy's HERstory

Sheriolyn M. Curry is inspirational. She is a CEO, a preacher, teacher, church planter, entrepreneur and life coach who loves watching lives transform. Her mission is to serve, empower others to use their God-given gifts, and to advance the kingdom of God. As a student of all things joyful, she goes by the social persona of "Dr. Joy."

In her early twenties, God called Sheriolyn to ministry. After a series of life events, including having a recurring dream over a twenty-year period, in 2003 she accepted the call. She was ordained an itinerant deacon in 2005 under Bishop John R. Bryant, and an itinerant elder in 2008 under Bishop T. Larry Kirkland. Sheriolyn earned a Master of Divinity from Fuller Theological Seminary in 2008.

Rev. Curry has held many leadership roles in the church, including youth minister, member of the Board of Trustees, finance committee, Board of Examiners and the Desert Mountain Conference Coordinator of Women in Ministry. Rev. Curry is the founding pastor of Mt. Moriah Community AME Church in Maricopa, AZ, and the former pastor of Greater Bethel AME Church in Phoenix, AZ. She currently serves as the presiding elder of the Rocky Mountain District in the Desert Mountain Conference, 5th Episcopal District, of the African Methodist Episcopal Church.

Since 2002, she has been the CEO and owner of several Comfort Keepers franchise offices, headquartered in Chandler, AZ. As a leading provider of non-medical home care services for senior adults, they are not only a first-thought provider for these types of services, but also educate and support families caring for loved ones in long-term care situations.

Sheriolyn has proven community leadership, having served on numerous boards and organizations, including Seeking Doors, Inc., Junior Achievement, and the African American Advisory Council for Congressional District 7 under Congressman Ruben Gallego. She is a charter member of the National Coalition of 100 Black Women Phoenix Metropolitan Chapter (2015); and a proud forty-four-year member of Alpha Kappa Alpha Sorority, Inc. She's received numerous leadership awards including the Positively Powerful Woman Award for Spiritual Leadership in 2012, and the NAACP 2016 Image Award for Religion, the Global Women's Summit Award for Leadership and the Desert Mountain Conference YPD Pastor of the Year.

Rev. Curry has an amazingly diverse, perfectly imperfect family. She has two daughters, four grandsons, and a host of bonus daughters and grandchildren. Siblings, nieces and nephews, cousins and an aunt round out her familial circle. In her free time, she loves to write, complete jigsaw puzzles and spend time with her grandchildren.

Her favorite scripture is Ephesians 3:20-21, "Now to him who is able to do far more abundantly than all that we ask, or think, according to the power at work within us, to him be glory in the church and in Christ Jesus throughout all generations, forever and ever."

Chapter 5
A Tale of Two Sisters: Leah and Rachel
(Genesis 29:16-30)
Dr. Sheriolyn Curry – aka "Dr. Joy"

Feeling unloved is a complex emotion, and at its core, it's a disconnect between how God sees us and how we see ourselves. As we are spiritual beings first, it is this human experience, where we interact with others, that causes the disconnect.

Feeling unloved is familiar to most of us. Unfortunately, we can easily get used to that feeling and even perpetuate it. Some of us throw great emotional "pity" parties. This is not to put anyone down who is going through something, but I want you to think about it. At your pity party event, the reasons you feel unloved are given credence; you invite the people who have hurt you to take up space in your mind, rehearse the situations where you were wronged, remember the times when you were rejected, abandoned, not included, picked last or otherwise mistreated. As you rewind and replay the unfavorable events of your life, the feeling of being unloved deepens. Your psyche is bombarded with all of this "evidence" and forgets the truth of who you really are, who you were made to be, and whose image you bear. The longer the pity party lasts, the more the negative emotions attach themselves to each other and to you, literally imprinting on your DNA. The more they bind together, the more they reinforce the notion of being unloved. When you awaken from this emotional pity party, *if* you awaken from it, you have been on such a roller coaster that you end up with a big emotional hangover. It's a vicious circle. All because we hold on to this false, albeit powerful, emotional narrative which says "You are unloved. You deserve to be unloved."

The Story of Two Sisters

The story of Leah and Rachel in Genesis 29:16-30 picks up at an interesting point in the text. Jacob had been working for Laban for about a month, when Laban asks him to name his wage for the work he's done. He didn't ask for money or livestock, he asked for Rachel, the one whom he loved.

In Genesis 29:16-20 (NRSV), we read, "Now Laban had two daughters; the name of the elder was Leah, and the name of the younger was Rachel. Leah's eyes were lovely, and Rachel was graceful and beautiful. Jacob loved Rachel; so he said, "I will serve you for seven years for your younger daughter Rachel." So, Jacob served seven years for Rachel and they seemed to him but a few days because of the love he had for her."

The love he had for her. Seven years in the making. And now it was time to marry her. The text continues in verses 21-30 with, "Then Jacob said to Laban, "Give me my wife that I may go in to her, for my time is completed." So Laban gathered together all the people of the place, and made a feast. But in the evening, he took his daughter Leah and brought her to Jacob; and he went in to her. (Laban gave his maid Zilpah to his daughter Leah to be her maid.) When morning came, it was Leah! And Jacob said to Laban, "What is this you have done to me? Did I not serve with you for Rachel? Why then have you deceived me?" Laban said, "This is not done in our country—giving the younger before the firstborn. Complete the week of this one, and we will give you the other also in return for serving me another seven years."

Can you imagine the humiliation Leah might have felt in that moment? Feeling not good enough, perhaps even used, and certainly unloved. Can you imagine Rachel's thoughts as she hears that she will be given to Jacob *if* he agrees to work seven more years for her father? And the humiliation she could have felt knowing that if this happens, she will always be wife number two?

What occurs when two sisters are thrust into a public rivalry not of their own choosing? When familial loyalty and cultural norms mandate your participation in a deceptive scheme, and secretly you are glad. After all, for most if not all your life you have been left out, made to feel less than, and even told your best features are your 'weak' eyes. Ha! That's like being described as just "having a good personality"! In many ways you may even feel that this is the only way to get what your heart desires—for someone to be tricked into loving you. What if, over time, the pervasive feeling of being unloved became your norm. You had long hidden your feelings of resentment, masked behind a narrative that you told yourself so many times, that you now believe you are unlovable? What do you do? Who do you turn to? Is it possible to retrain your mind to quell the outside noise and know for certain that you are indeed loveable and worthy of love.

Although the Bible is silent on what the relationship between Leah and Rachel was like during those seven years, from the time periods including the week Leah had Jacob to herself, and life after Rachel married Jacob, we can conclude from further reading that indeed, things had changed between these two sisters. Can't you see how the seeds of competition, jealousy, envy and doubt have not only been planted, but watered and taken root? Loved versus unloved. This opposition generates powerful, complicated emotions resulting in complex, and sometimes unloving behaviors. Following are four views on this situation: two from the sisters, one from the writer, and one from the Creator. Prayerfully, this will help us all understand God's love for His people. His is a love that goes far beyond human capacity.

Rachel's View

Hi, I'm Rachel. Many of you know me from the story in Genesis as Leah's younger sister, the pretty one. You probably think you know all about me from what is described as my story, but do you really know what it was like to be 'me'? Let me share with you what it was like growing up as the "pretty younger sister". First of all, my daddy, Laban, was a protector, typical for men in our culture and time period. He worked hard and did the best he could with what we had, wanting to make sure his family was taken care of, especially us girls. At least until he could marry us off. He used to tell me that he wasn't as worried about me because of how I looked and knew how to take care of the livestock, so I would have my choice of suitors. I would nod and smile in agreement, but secretly I wondered if I would have any choice in who my husband would be, and how many children I would give him. Really, how many sons, because that's what was most valued in our culture.

Early on, I felt loved by my daddy and my brothers. But they would always use that 'pretty' word. Come here 'pretty girl'. Or what's for dinner 'pretty girl'? Your husband will love you, 'pretty girl'. I began to think that to be lovable meant that you only had to look a certain way and that was it. But, if that were true, did that mean they didn't love my sister, Leah? I never heard them call her 'pretty girl'. Is she unlovable? Did she do something to make them not love her? Or, maybe it was what she didn't do. I decided right then and there that I wanted to be loved, so I was going to do whatever it took to keep that feeling alive!

My sister, Leah, was smart and thoughtful, and somehow didn't seem to care if she was loved or not! She just did what she was supposed to do around the house and being the older sister, she was asked to do a lot! She took care of me although I wasn't always nice to her. I was just following what others said and did to her. She acted more like my mother than my sister. But she didn't complain about it. Well, if she did, she didn't complain out loud. You want to know something that was strange? She talked to God... a lot. What was that about?

Since pretty was the lens that I would use to judge whether someone deserved to be loved, I devoted a lot of time to my looks and the way I walked and talked. I focused on outside beauty. As a teenager, not only was I a 'looker', but I also had developed what you would call graceful ways.

One day, as I was shepherding my father's sheep, I came upon a relative, Jacob, my Aunt Rebekah's son. I ran and told my daddy, and he came out, greeted Jacob and brought him to our house. Even though we heard he had done something deceitful to his brother, he was kinfolk and needed a place to stay so he stayed with us. About a month passed and I knew that Jacob had fallen in love with me. Ha, ha and he couldn't take his eyes off of me. Daddy said there'd be days like this!

He and my father made some kind of deal where Jacob would work for him as a hired hand for seven years in exchange for marrying me! Over the next seven years we saw a lot of each other while we worked with the flock and then back at the house since he stayed with us. Near the end of the seven years, my father called my sister and me together and told us that I would not be the one going into the marriage chambers at the wedding, but that he was giving Leah to Jacob! Say, what? Wait a minute. After all this time, I'm not getting married? I'm the pretty one. I'm the one he wants, the one he loves. I was not happy with that decision at all, but my father had laid down the law. It was final. And I couldn't even tell Jacob. I wouldn't disobey my father, but I could give my sister an earful. Initially she didn't know what to say, other than "you know that's our custom," or "it was Dad's decision." Like she had nothing to do with it. I bet she started all of this. She had this fake smile on her face like she was so sorry. Boy, was I mad! That's when things between my sister and me began to change.

Leah's View

My name is Leah, and I am Rachel's older sister. Where shall I start? First, let it be known that I love my family, and I am fiercely loyal to them. But sometimes they say some hurtful things to me. They like to focus on the fact that I didn't look as good as my sister, Rachel, and talked about it *all of the time*. Ha, ha…not funny anymore! They don't even notice my other qualities. I am smart, faithful, and loyal. I respect my elders and I know I would be a good wife. Surely these qualities count for something. Surely this makes one loveable.

You want to know something funny? My name in Hebrew means "delicate; weary". It's funny to me because I seem to have fought all my life to appear strong, to fight off the insecurities that come from being unloved. I prayed to God about all of this. Actually, talked to him a lot. That's where my fortitude came from. I might not have outside beauty, but I have inner strength!

My family is religious and follows ancient customs where daughters are concerned. The girls tend the house, but we also help my brothers with the animals. My sister, Rachel, is a shepherdess. That means that she tends the flocks and takes them to the watering spot. It was there that our cousin, Jacob, saw her and revealed who he was. The next thing I knew, Jacob is staying with us. I could tell he had fallen for my sister. A woman knows these things. But it was a surprise when he asked my daddy if he could have her in marriage, and in exchange would work as my father's hired hand for seven years! He must really love her. I was happy for my sister and prayed that I would know love like that one day.

Well, as the story goes, the seven years went by rather quickly and Jacob was ready for the marriage to be consummated. My father had decided that he would use our cultural norms to trick Jacob and that I, the oldest sister, would be the one marrying him, not Rachel! Now mind you, he didn't tell Jacob this, but Rachel knew. There is no way we could have pulled this off and she not know about it. We were obedient daughters. When my father decided that's what would happen, regardless of how we felt about it, that's the way it was going to be. All

80

of the time she had spent waiting, planning and dreaming of being Jacob's wife was for naught. Now I was going to have her man. I could tell that she was hot!

Initially, I didn't know what to say to her. I thought it was because I felt sorry for her, but soon realized it was because I was happy for myself! Secretly I felt this was the only way I would get married; someone would have to be tricked into doing so. The fact that my father spearheaded this made it somewhat acceptable, after all I am the older sister. This decision gave me a new level of confidence. I can't explain it, but I no longer felt like I had to be 'nice' to my sister and that this was poetic justice for all the times she wasn't nice to me. Finally, I would have someone to love me. My husband would have to love me. And, I would have lots of male children for him. Yes, I am lovable. I am worthy of love and my father made sure of it! I could hardly contain myself. And that's when things really changed between me and my sister.

The custom was to throw a big feast, then the wife is brought to the marriage bed. Well, another part of the custom is that the woman is completely veiled when brought to the groom. So, in I went. I still wonder how, after all the time they had been around each other, Jacob didn't know I wasn't Rachel! We consummated the marriage that night. I never felt love like that...but it was short-lived.

The next morning when Jacob discovered it was me, he was not happy—much different from the night before (ahem). He confronted my dad, "Why did you trick me?" he said. My dad explained our custom and made another deal with him. If he completed the honeymoon week with me, then he could have Rachel as well, providing he worked another seven years for my father. So, at the end of the seven days, we both were married to Jacob. Now it was a race to see which one of us he would love more. Which one would give him the most children. Which one of us would...you get the picture. The rivalry between sisters can be fierce. But you can read about that in Chapter 9.

My Story

I think in many ways most if not all of us can identify with a feeling of being unloved, or unworthy of real love. As a child growing up in a household of five children, I often felt out of place. I am the middle child, and the middle girl. I have two sisters, one five years older and one five years younger. I looked different. My interests were different. I was just different. At one point I asked my mother where she got me from because I surely couldn't have been born into this family. Admitting that was difficult because I really loved them.

As an adult looking back in time, I don't have memories of hanging out with my older sister, or my younger sister hanging out with me. We grew up in the same house, but separately. We had different journeys. Unbeknownst to me there were undercurrents of sibling rivalry fueling our interactions, you know, passive-aggressive behavior, which surfaced later in life.

My mom made sure we were cared for. My dad was in my life until I was about five years old, and then he wasn't. There was no explanation; he was just gone. I didn't find out until decades later that it was because he had another family. And although I don't remember being told that I was unloved, I seemed to have a hard time accepting that I was loved, no matter who said it. I remember at five years old feeling abandoned and rejected but didn't have words to express my complex emotions. I guess my dad no longer 'loved' me. The remedy was to focus on things that made me feel good—like school and church.

Even in school I was different. From the time I started school, I really liked going and hungered for more to do. The teachers loved that about me, the students, not so much. And to add to the mix that I went to a predominantly Black elementary school and was the lightest complected child in the school. Actually, me and one other girl, but she had freckles in her face, so she looked "darker". Kids used to chase me home from school calling me "light bright" and taunted me because I was tall. Was I that unlovable? Clearly, they didn't 'love' me.

I started going to church when I was nine years old. I heard stories about a God who loves all of us so much that he offered his Son's life in exchange for whoever would believe in Him (John 3:16). It didn't matter what I did wrong in the past, I could be forgiven if I just asked. And, I didn't have to act a certain way, be a certain skin tone or have fame or status. And by simply asking, I could live with God forever when I died. I just needed to believe. God loved me that much!

Such a pure love was foreign to me. My everyday existence still had people treating me as "unloved" and me feeling "unlovable." I craved to know that kind of love, so I kept going back. Eventually, I gave my life to Christ—I became a believer.

In the presence of the Lord is where I felt unconditional love. It was there that I also learned to give unconditional love. It was easy to extend it to others, but not so easy to give it to myself. When you've lived a life feeling unloved, you tend to focus on your "supposed" faults. The tender place within us where there has been a painful exposure will have us feeling inadequate, guilty, or ashamed. It leaves us constantly trying to make up for the flaws, to prove our worth. As a child it is hard to recognize and accept that the disappointment you feel is due to an inadequacy in the adult and not the child. How many of us have rationalized away someone's poor behavior and made it about something lacking in us? These misplaced feelings developed as a child are often carried into adulthood.

God's View

The Bible is full of verses about love. For those who believe in God and follow the teachings of Christ, love takes on a whole new meaning. Over and over again we are told to love one another (1 John 4:11). To love others (our neighbors) as we love ourselves (Mark 12:31). To love the Lord our God with all our heart, soul and mind (Mark 12:29-30). God is the ultimate love force. His very essence is love. God loves us even when we don't love ourselves. When others withhold love, God's love is ever-present. God's love is a constant reminder that He is with us, He hears us, and He sees us. It's comforting, protecting, and everlasting. It never gives out, gives up or gives in.

Isaiah 54:10 TM says "'For even if the mountains walk away and the hills fall to pieces, my love won't walk away from you, my covenant commitment of peace won't fall apart.' The God who has compassion on you says so." Because God loves you so much, you are also capable of loving in deeper and stronger ways each day (Ephesians 3:18-19). God has given us the Holy Spirit to fill our hearts with love (Romans 5:5). This will help us show love to others even if in our earthly viewpoint, they don't deserve it. As humans we look for reasons to love and find reasons not to love. But God's love is beyond reason. I think that is what makes it so remarkable. It is only when we begin to comprehend God's love, which goes beyond knowledge, that we begin to be filled with all the fullness of God (Ephesians 3:19).

One of the things that is said of Leah is that she talked to God often. I'm not surprised. I can hear her pouring out her anguish about being unloved. Can you imagine what it was like for her when the love of God washed over her, and she realized that no matter what people said, or did, or didn't do, it would never separate her from God's love? What strength that gave her! Dieter F. Uchtdorf wrote, "Though we are incomplete, God loves us completely. Though we are imperfect, God loves us perfectly. Though we may feel lost and without a compass, God's love encompasses us completely...He loves every one of us, even those who are flawed, rejected, awkward, sorrowful or broken."

God loves us *not* because we are lovable, but because He is love. Not because He needs to receive, because *he* delights to give. (C.S. Lewis). So, to all of the Leahs and Rachels and Sheriolyns out there, know this: *God loves you*! It is my prayer that as you stay in God's presence, as you bask in the fullness of who He is, that you will let nothing separate you from His love. You see, *unloved* is simply not in God's vocabulary.

Chapter 6

Leah's Misery: Now Jacob Will Love Me
(Genesis 29: 31-32)
Latoia Russell-Williams

Latoia's HERstory

Evangelist Latoia Russell-Williams is a licensed minister with the Pentecostal Churches of the Apostolic Faith Incorporated, and a collaborative author in this soon-to-be bestseller book *Unloved*.

Evangelist Russell-Williams is the baby girl of Ms. Ruby Crosby and Mr. Emanuel L. Russell. Her Christian journey began in a small church on the "Hill" in Joliet, where she grew up. She faithfully attended every church service and anything else the church sponsored with her grandmother, Sis. Jerlene Crosby. Sometimes her attendance was voluntary and sometimes it was involuntary, nevertheless, she went. As she grew older, she eventually developed a love for God and His people. It was in her early teenage years that she felt God calling her to the ministry. However, after running from God like a track star, and many epic fails in life, she came to herself and submitted to the will of God. In her late thirties, she accepted the call God had placed on her life.

After her former pastor transitioned, she became a member of Christ Temple Apostolic Faith Church in Joliet, IL under the leadership of the P.C.A.F.I. former Presiding Prelate Bishop J.E. Moore. It was under this leadership that she attended Bell Bible College and graduated from the Evangelistic Training Association. She currently serves at her local assembly as a minister, Sisterhood treasurer, event coordinator, choir member, youth Bible Study instructor, on the Altar Evangelism Team member, Praise Team member and Cleaning Committee member.

The Lord has gifted Evangelist Russell-Williams with an abundance of talents that she executes with a spirit of excellence. She enjoys sewing, cooking, decorating, singing, and designing publications for the church and her community. She served for many years as an Intermediate Sunday School teacher, developing one of the largest classes in the Sunday School department. She has a heart for young people and desires to see them grow in God.

God gifted her with her only child, her heartbeat, a beautiful baby girl, Kailyn D. Russell. As a single mom she went back to college to be an example to her daughter that education was important. It was not until after she met James F. Williams, Jr. that she realized what love really was between a man and a woman. They became best friends, praise buddies and prayer partners. One of her greatest joys was marrying her best friend and love of her life in June of 2020. To this union James gained one daughter, and Russell-Williams gained four beautiful daughters; Chanell Chambers, Jasmin Williams, Jalissa Williams and Mykel Stewart-Williams, all of whom she loves as her very own. She currently has seven amazing grandchildren and two beautiful great- granddaughters.

If Evangelist Russell-Williams ever felt unloved, her family and her dedication to God and church service have proven to that love still exists, and God has His hand on her life. It is her heart's desire to do the will of the father as she serves God and his people. One of her favorite scriptures is Psalm 139:14: *I will praise thee; for I am fearfully and wonderfully made: marvelous are thy works; and that my soul knoweth right well.*

Chapter 6
Leah's Misery: Now Jacob Will Love Me
(Genesis 29: 31-32)
Latoia Russell-Williams

Misery is defined as a state or feeling of great distress, or discomfort of mind or body. The word is derived from the Latin word *miseria*, from miser, meaning wretched, great mental or emotional distress, or *extreme* unhappiness.

The Courtship
A period during which a couple develop a romantic relationship, especially with a view to marriage.

The moment they saw each other butterflies began to flutter in their stomachs. There was almost an immediate and intense emotional connection. A certain amount of excitement filled their hearts, causing big smiles to cross their faces. He couldn't seem to get enough of her, and she couldn't seem to get enough of him. They exchanged numbers and talked for hours about everything and nothing. Sometimes just listening to each other breathe was sufficient, until the next time they could be in each other's presence.

Doesn't this sound like the typical beginning of any relationship? As time progresses descriptive words like "really like" and "love" are introduced into the relationship, to describe how one person feels about the other.

Jacob loved Rachel the moment he laid his eyes on her. It was truly love at first sight. He knew like most men when he first saw her that he wanted her to be his wife. Jacob had purposed in his mind to do whatever it took to make Rachel his. But first, he had to ask her father, Laban, for her hand in marriage. Laban, being Jacob's mother's brother, felt there was no better person to give Rachel to than a family member. Leah, on the other hand, being the eldest daughter was unmarried as well. It was their custom that the oldest daughter marries before the youngest daughter. Laban knew what he planned to do was not according to the tradition of their culture, but out of his deceitfulness he was willing to sell or barter his daughters for Jacob's labor.

Here it is that his nephew who wants to marry his youngest daughter, his oldest daughter is still unmarried, and he has work in the field to be done. So, Laban comes up with this great idea. He figures out a way to solve all three of his problems at one time. In the midst of Laban's decision-making, Leah's happiness was completely disregarded. It was as if her feelings or concerns didn't matter, as if she was a non-factor in this life changing plan. For Leah, dating was not an option and romance was never even considered. She was robbed of the experience of being found, being chased and courted. Later we learn that this created a condition of suffering for Leah known as misery.

The Wedding
A marriage ceremony, especially considered as including the associated celebrations.

Most women have always dreamed of one day being a bride. The dream likely started well before the reality of marriage ever presented itself. Some women mentally start planning their wedding as a little girl. They pick their favorite colors, favorite flower, and begin picturing themselves in a pretty pearl and diamond embellished gown. They have an idea of when and where they want their wedding to be located. The fun part is picking all of the friends that they want to include in the wedding. Many little girls are so detailed they have an idea of what their *Prince Charming* will look like, and how many kids they want to have. They even know the type of house they want and choose a name for the dog or cat. She only needs to wait for time to pass so that she can grow up and live out the perfect wedding, the perfect life, and her happily ever after.

A wedding is a special and joyous occasion that calls for careful planning and execution. Usually someone is hired to help coordinate the details, so that the bride won't have so much to worry about. Someone is designated to attend to the bride and assist her in getting ready since this is her day. I know that the groom is important, but let's keep it real, it's really all about the bride on the wedding day. Everything is just right—her hair, nails, shoes, and even the undergarments so that her dress enhances her curves the right way.

Something old, something new, and something blue have been selected. Everyone is in the right place, and the music is cued at the right time. The groom arrives early and stands in his spot, patiently waiting. Parents are in place, along with grandparents; ushers are staged and the bridal party is ready to go. Then the doors are closed so that the bride can make her grand entrance.

This is the entrance that she's been dreaming of making as a little girl, the entrance that will leave everyone in awe of her beauty. Will the groom shed a tear in disbelief at how gorgeous she is, and the fact that she will be all his? Well, that's the "wow" effect we're going for. It's time. The perfect song is playing for the perfect day and the perfect bride. The doors open, everyone stands, and the bride comes into view. She is almost blinded by the flurry of camera flashes. People clap and cheer as she stands at the top of the aisle holding on to her father's arm. She catches a glimpse of her Prince Charming wiping his eyes. Yes, mission "wow effect" accomplished. Can't you feel the love between the bride and groom, the way he looks at her so passionately. Can you imagine how lovely and romantic the dimly lit sanctuary ceremony was? Now, off to the reception venue. The music and the food are top notch, laughter fills the air, and you can still feel the love in the room. Everyone is having a great time.

Your wedding became the talk of the town. You were the perfect bride, stunning and beautiful, and you married the perfect man. He is loved by everyone; your dad considers him a son and your husband calls your mother mom. At this point, what could possibly go wrong?

* * *

Leah's wedding day was nothing like what was customary during her time, or what we experience today. She didn't get to wear a fancy gown, she didn't get all dolled up for her husband to create the "wow" effect. She did have a big feast which is comparable to what we know as a reception, but she wasn't even honored. You see, the reality is that Jacob was working all those years, seven to be exact, to marry Leah's little sister Rachel. You know Rachel, the one that the Bible describes as "beautiful and well favoured" (Genesis 29:17). Leah, the oldest, was described in that same passage of scripture as being "tender-eyed" or "weak". What a description, and what a way to compare two sisters. It was as if one sister was better than the other, or because Leah wasn't as pretty as Rachel she was to be thought less than and treated as inferior.

Leah's dad played a major role in this fiasco of a wedding. He

90

tricked Jacob into marrying her. Laban, in his deceitful selfish ways traded his own daughter in exchange for free manual labor from Jacob. He betrayed his nephew and went back on his word. The agreement was for Rachel and Jacob wakes up to Leah. Jacob, being a deceiver himself, has now been deceived but at the cost of Leah's heart.

Leah now realizes that her dad does not really love her or thinks that she will never find love because of how she looks. This is why he was convinced he needed to trick a man into marrying her. Then the man that she married does not love her because he wants her little sister. Leah is faced with rejection on every side. Can you imagine how low her self-esteem must have been? Can you imagine the mental and emotional misery she must have felt coming to terms with these realities?

The Disillusionment
A feeling of disappointment resulting from the discovery that something is not as good as one believed it to be.

The honeymoon is over, and you have arrived at your new home as husband and wife. It's time to unpack and get settled. This new journey together is going to be amazing. You love each other and nothing can separate you. As you start to unpack you make a mental checklist, trying to be the best wife and alleviate any pressure off of the mister. All the clothes on hangers are hung up and the clothes in the drawers are folded and towels are put away neatly in the linen closet. The dishes are washed, and the kitchen is spotless. The responsibilities have been set, he knows what he's responsible for and she knows what she's responsible for. Whoever gets home first is responsible for starting dinner. Teamwork makes the dream work. As time goes on you become comfortable with each other so you become a little more relaxed and not so pressured to impress your mate. You leave the seat up and she falls in the toilet at night. She gets mad and dries your t-shirts now it looks like all your shirts are too small. Now the real you begins to show up and the representative leaves the scene. The arguments start happening more frequently and some hurtful things are being said in the heat of the moment. And just when you think you have experienced it all you wake up to someone you don't know. Her hair is on the dresser, her eyelashes are next to her hair along with three of her nails. His teeth are sitting on the sink in the master bathroom and his underwear is on the floor in front of the dirty clothes basket. You think, *wait what did I sign up for?* Now that you're married you find out that you don't agree on how the children should be raised, how bills should be paid, religion or anything else. His sisters don't like you and your brothers don't like him. Wait, when did all this come about? Everything is changing so quickly. This was supposed to be the perfect marriage. He's the perfect man for me, I'm the perfect woman for him. This is not how I ever envisioned my life turning out, especially my marriage, but I love him.

> *"And it came to pass, that in the morning, behold, it was Leah: and he said to Laban, <u>what is this thou hast done unto me</u>? did not I serve with thee for Rachel? Wherefore then has thou beguiled me?" —Genesis 29:25 KJV*

Jacob wakes up angry that he is not with the woman he worked for, the woman he was promised, but instead her "not so pretty" older sister. Laban had arranged for his daughter to be with a man who openly expressed that he did not want her and did not love her. He was so angry that he referred to her *and* their marriage as "this", as if she was not even human or as if she was beneath him. Was it because Leah's eyes were not as beautiful as Rachel's? Was it because she was not as beautiful to look at or her complexion as pretty as Rachel's? Was it because Jacob had already kissed Rachel at the well? Whatever the case, Leah's father, Laban, saw an opportunity to get Jacob to work for free seven more years, and out of Jacob's intense desire and love for Rachel, he agreed.

> *"And he went in also unto Rachel, and he loved also Rachel more than Leah, and served with him yet seven other years." —Genesis 29:30*

The rejection, disrespect, hurt, pain, and betrayal by Leah's father, husband and sister is so intense that most women would have killed Jacob in his sleep and vowed to never speak to their father ever again. This is enough to completely deplete any woman of her self-worth, self-esteem, confidence, or her ability to walk away from what is essentially causing her extreme unhappiness. It is not recorded that Jacob was physically abusive to her, but he was definitely hazardous to

Leah's health. Leah may have been Jacob's first wife, but she was not his first choice. This is enough to make any woman bitter.

The Misery

A state or feeling of great distress or discomfort of mind or body. A state of suffering and want that is a result of poverty.

The Bible doesn't go into great detail about Leah's mindset, but some things are implied. Leah had the same physical, emotional and psychological experiences as women across the world have today. I believe she longed to be loved by her father and her husband. After all the first man that a little girl typically learns to love is her father. He's the first example of what a man is and how he should treat a woman. She pays close attention to how her father interacts with her mother. Does he open the door, does he openly express his love to her or does he appear emotionless and standoff-ish? Does he speak with love or is his tone always harsh and abrasive. Most little girls grow up wanting a man that has traits and characteristics like or similar to their father. When Leah married Jacob she truly did marry a man with the same characteristics as her father Laban, deceitful and conniving.

In Leah's case she wanted Jacob to love her. Leah wanted to experience the same type of love that Isaac had for Rebekah or the type of love expressed in the Song of Solomon. Because of Jacob's burning desire for Rachel, he undervalued Leah. He disregarded her worth as a woman and even worse, as his wife.

"And he went also unto Rachel, and he loved also Rachel more than Leah, and served with him yet seven other years." - Genesis 29:30

Jacob continued to sleep with Leah the entire seven years he worked for her father in exchange for marrying Rachel.

"And when the Lord saw that Leah was hated, he opened her womb: but Rachel was barren." - Genesis 29:31

Leah continued to have baby after baby, thinking that it would cause Jacob to love her. When she didn't get the response she wanted from Jacob, she allowed him to have children by her handmaid. Leah, like many women today, felt that if she had a baby, especially a son, she

93

would capture Jacob's heart and he would somehow fall in love with her.

> *"And Leah conceived, and bare a son, and she called his name Reuben: for she said, Surely the Lord hath looked upon my affliction; now therefore my husband will love me." —Genesis 29:32*

Can you imagine the mental anguish Leah must have felt to watch her husband cater to her sister? As if she was only good enough to lay with and have his children. Leah was emotionally deprived and neglected. The depth of psychological pain cannot be imagined. The pain that comes with chasing Jacob emotionally, while he chased Rachel emotionally and physically. Every time he laid with Leah he created another emotional tie, drawing in her feelings and emotions deeper every time.

Could it be possible that Leah played a major role in her own misery? Leah entered into the marital covenant with Jacob knowing that the plan was to deceive him. Her father Laban was the mastermind behind the awful scheme of deception but Leah at some point could have warned Jacob. She did not have to go along with the plan or continue with the lie. Leah had a chance to come clean with Jacob; once she became his wife she was no longer under her father's command. There is a part of me that feels like Leah knew her chances to marry were slim to none. She didn't possess the beauty that her sister had and she, too, saw an opportunity to profit from the scheme. After the marriage, when Laban took Leah to Jacob, she kept her face concealed until after the marriage was consummated. Nothing good can come out of a lie. Love cannot abide where deception, hatred, lies, greed, and envy reside. Is it possible that Jacob resented Leah for being a part of her father's lie?

The Awakening
An act or moment of becoming suddenly aware of something.

What part did you play in your failed relationship? Did you play the victim or did you honestly ask yourself "What was my role in the breakdown of the relationship?" What could you have done to save it?

Did you give it your very best? Did you do the work to make sure that if the relationship failed it was not because you did not try? Have you accepted the reality of your current situation?

> *"And when Rachel saw that she bare Jacob no children, Rachel envied her sister; and said unto Jacob, give me children, or else I die." —Genesis 30:1*

The beautiful and fair complected Rachel envied her tender-eyed, wretched, older sister Leah. Envy is defined as the distress or resentment we feel when others have what we don't. Envy is feeling grievous about the good of another— no sin is more offensive to God, nor more injurious to our neighbor or ourselves. Rachel's distress and anguish of being barren was enough to make her want to die. Jacob is so outraged at Rachel, he asks the question:

> *"Am I in God's stead, who hath withheld from thee the fruit of the womb?" —Genesis 30:2*

Jacob scolded Rachel; he openly expressed his anger and displeasure by asking her if he was greater than God, who was he to give her what God had denied her. Rachel finally meets reality and tries everything in her power to satisfy Jacob with having a son. She wanted to be favored more than Leah. She knew it was a blessing to be able to have children. She even indirectly suggested that she was in competition with her sister Leah.

> *"And Rachel said, with great wrestlings have I wrestled with my sister, and I have prevailed." —Genesis 30:8*

Rachel envied her sister so much that she gave her handmaid Bilhah to Jacob to produce children on her behalf. Leah played into this madness and gave Jacob two more sons and a daughter, making it a total of seven children. Leah awakened to her reality in Genesis chapter 29 verse 35:

> *"And she conceived again, and bore a son: and she said, now will I praise the Lord: therefore she called his name Judah; and left bearing."*

Leah knew she didn't have the looks and in her desperate quest to get Jacob to love her she named her first three sons out of her misery. The first son was named Reuben meaning "see, a son", her second son was named Simeon meaning "to hear, listen", her third son was named Levi meaning "joined". This was her ultimate expectation, to be joined with Jacob, but something happened when she had her fourth son Judah meaning "praise". There was a shift in Leah's mindset which caused her to change the way she viewed things, ultimately causing her to change her reaction to Jacob's actions. "Now will I praise the Lord" indicates that she has surrendered to the will of God because everything that she tried to do to get Jacob to love her did not work. It was an epic fail. Because Leah reverenced God and her husband, God opened her womb. It still didn't change the fact that her husband did not love her, but she developed a relationship with God. When her mindset changed about her reality, she was able to put a praise on depression, neglect, deprivation, loneliness, hatred, bitterness, shame, self-defeat, low self-esteem, mental anguish, self-pity, remorse and any other negative spirit she encountered. Her situation did not change, but in the midst of her current situation she began to praise God.

When we praise God in the midst of our situations and circumstances it uncovers the many ways God blesses us on a daily basis. He graciously gives us grace and mercy to overcome obstacles. He makes ways out of no way, He protects us when we aren't even aware of danger, He regulates our minds, He gives us a garment of praise for the spirit of heaviness. Praise is an outward expression of our gratitude for the things God has done for us. Praise was and still is the order for the day.

Leah's misery was not to her demise; her latter was greater than her beginning. I believe once Jacob realized how wicked Rachel's heart was and how she envied her sister, he was able to see past Rachel's beauty. I believe his heart grew fond of Leah over time, never loving her like he loved Rachel but more than he did when he first married her. In the end, Jacob saw that when Leah passed away, she had a proper burial and he was to be buried next to her. All the discomfort and agony Leah felt was not in vain. She was the mother of royalty and the high priest, she was the mother of the Davidic dynasty and the lineage of our Lord and Savior Jesus Christ. Leah raised her children to be leaders.

She did not let her relationship with Jacob detour her from her motherly or wifely duties. She stayed the course to the very end and as we can see she reaped the benefits of being faithful despite what her husband did. There are so many lessons to be learned from Leah.

One, God's view and plan for our life goes beyond what the natural eye can see.

"For I know the thoughts that I think toward you, saith the Lord, thoughts of peace, and not of evil, to give you an expected end." —Jeremiah 29:11

Two, our reaction to our current situation cannot stem from anger. We must remain humble in every area and circumstance in our life. When we do things out of bitterness or with the intent to harm, hurt or cause grief to others it usually ends up causing us grief. Leah did not try to get back at her father Laban, her husband Jacob, or her sister Rachel. How many of us can honestly say we would have stayed and continued to be a "good" wife to Jacob?

"The aged women likewise, that [they be] in behaviour as becometh holiness, not false accusers, not given to much wine, teachers of good things; That they may teach the young women to be sober, to love their husbands, to love their children, [To be] discreet, chaste, keepers at home, good, obedient to their own husbands, that the word of God be not blasphemed." —Titus 2:3-5

Last but not least, Leah teaches us how important it is to have a relationship with God and how to be content. Even though her relationship with Jacob was loveless, she continued to cry out to God with her request. In her conversations with God, she came to realize that her cries didn't go unanswered. God didn't answer them the way she wanted, but her suffering, her discomfort of mind, her misery didn't go unnoticed. God reassured Leah that He heard her and favored her when He opened her womb and allowed her to bear children. Contentment or the ability to be free from care because of satisfaction with what is already one's own whatever it may be is not a favorable state to most humans. The world applies pressure to do better, get more, get bigger or better but Leah came to a point where she was satisfied with what she had and where she was since she had no control, but she trusted her God to make everything all right. Leah's faith wasn't in man but God. When she was awakened to the reality that Jacob may never love her, she was able to move past how he felt about her and see how much God loved her. Her blessings became her avenue to say thank you to God for all He had done for her. She came to a place in her life where her praise became bigger than her problem. Leah's contentment brought her a peace that man was unable to comprehend.

> *"For I reckon that the sufferings of this present time [are] not worthy [to be compared] with the glory which shall be revealed in us" —Romans 8:18*

I would like to encourage every reader, despite your current situation or state of being, to make peace with God and find peace in God. Misery has become a common state of being for many people. There was a period of my life when I was most miserable. I began to neglect myself and feel depressed. I tried to keep it together so people would not know what I was experiencing but it came to a point where my misery had prominent physical effects on me. My eyes were likened to Leah's eyes they were tired and weak from all the tears that I had shed over the days and the months. I continued to go to church, take care of the house, attend meetings, preach the Gospel, pray for others to be healed and delivered all while I was in desperate need of God to deliver me. I will never forget when God clearly spoke to me. I was in the shower and I heard Him say "change your reaction" I looked around as if someone was in the shower with me. I have to admit I failed horribly at obeying the voice of the Lord. I thought I was "changing" my reaction, but when I began to honestly assess what I'd been doing I realized I hadn't changed at all. So, through much prayer and transparent moments, tears and heartache I finally got it. Just like natural school, life's school is full of testing periods, so the test presented itself again and it was up to me to pass. I changed my reaction, and I was able to see the benefits of obedience to God as He stepped in and began to work in my favor.

Some people are content with being miserable but God's plan for our lives does not include misery. Yes, there may be times of discomfort but it's not permanent, it's only for a moment. I felt like my situation was never going to change but I stayed the course and continued, as my husband says, to keep my side of the street clean. Like

Leah I felt unloved, abandoned, forgotten and even hated by God. But God reminded me how much He loved me. I began to count all the many blessings that I had as well as how much worse my situation could have been versus what was really going on. I began to repent for thinking that God who is rich in mercy, grace and love could hate me. God heard my cry just as He heard Leah's cry and just like He will hear yours. Change your mind and you will change your life, continue to pray and never cease. Decide to praise God no matter what and be content in the state that you are in until God delivers you.

"...and she said, Now will I praise the Lord..." Genesis 29:35

Chapter 7

God's Compensation for Rejection: Leah's Fertile Years
(Genesis 29:33-35)
Katrina Washington, Bridal Consulting, Medical Assistant

Katrina's HERstory

Katrina Washington received her local ministerial fellowship certification through the Midwest District Council P.A.W. in 2013. She served as an active member and evangelist under the leadership of District Elder Allan E. Rudd, Sr. at Lively Stone Apostolic Church of Mount Vernon, IL. She has served as a minister, praise team member, outreach team member, street minister, prison minister, healthcare coordinator, prayer leader and warrior, overseer, fund raiser, committee leader, pastoral aide, armor bearer and event coordinator. She has privately cared for many saints, been rewarded for her service, and established strong networks within the community.

"That thine alms may be in secret: and thy Father which seeth in secret himself shall reward thee openly - Matthew 6:4

In 2016, Katrina received an honorable minister ordination by the Christian National Church Minister Outreach Program. She relocated to the Chicagoland area and obtained membership at Grace & Glory Apostolic Church in Zion, IL. Under the leadership of Pastor Elder Dennis Broom, she served as an evangelist, church housekeeper, and Sunday school teacher. She was brought up in holiness and attended Indiana Avenue Pentecostal Church of God in Chicago, IL, which is known to many as "35th Street," under the leadership of the Honorable and late Bishop Charles E. Davis. Since his passing she decided to be a blessing to the ministry and return to serve the kingdom of God in the very place upon which her foundation was built. She has made-up her mind that she wants to live so that God can use her in any capacity. Currently she serves in the healthcare professionals ministry.

"Train up a child in the way he should go: and when he is old, he will not depart from it." - Proverbs 22:6

Katrina has been entrepreneurial since childhood. In 2010 she started a wedding planning business, which today is named "The Prayer Warriors on Purpose." Katrina is also the founder and leader of "The Prayer Warriors on Purpose" Intercessor Prayer Warrior Team. She is a prayer warrior and intercessor, and her prayer team consistently prays for the nation. Her outreach ministry, originally Order My Steps Ministries, is now "DBA" Fresh Start Ministries & Events. Katrina has a gift of helps and is always willing to lend a helping hand and she has a passion for advocating on others' behalf.

Katrina is the author of a global novel called "Thee Black Marker," for which she had her first live radio show interview on WRLR 98.3 FM "The Voice of Lake County". Since then, she has been interviewed on television and her book has can be found in libraries and bookstore shelves. Journalism was her major in college, but life happened, and she didn't pursue it immediately, yet her faith didn't fail her. Eventually she came full circle and the Lord opened the door for her to host her very own radio show. Today she is radio personality Ms. Katrina Monique on "The Single, Saved & Successful" inspirational show. Katrina is a member of the Grayslake Arts Alliance, and has been a reporter on several episodes of Mr. Elroy Reed's "The Peoples Voice of Lake County" newscast.

"The people that do know their God shall be strong; and do exploits. - *Daniel 11:32*

Katrina is purpose driven and loves God's people. She has a heart for the homeless, believes that if you want to see a change you must be the change that you want to see, and that it is better to give than to receive. She has coordinated a fundraiser that served hundreds of families and manages a pen-pal ministry that serves nursing facilities and prisons. She is a staple during events to feed the homeless, at food pantries and during prayer walks. Evangelist Katrina doesn't limit herself; she stretches her faith. She loves to write and read and uses her gifts to bless others.

Evangelist Katrina graduated from cosmetology and medical assistant schools and has successfully completed an Emergency Medical Technician program; she has practiced as a certified nurse assistant for over 10 years and has an honorary degree as a bridal consultant. Katrina recently completed The School of Preach. She has four beautiful, intelligent, and healthy children, and four adorable grandchildren. Katrina knows that she does not look like what she has been through, including a life-threatening doctor's report. She has a radical praise and has a right to praise Him like she does.

"I will praise thee; for I am fearfully and wonderfully made; marvelous are thy works and that my soul knoweth right well." - *Psalm 139:14*

Chapter 7
God's Compensation for Rejection: Leah's Fertile Years
(Genesis 29:33-35)
Katrina Washington

"She conceived again, and bare a son; and said, Because the LORD hath heard I was hated, he hath therefore given me this son also: and she called his name Simeon. And she conceived again, and bare a son; and said, now this time will my husband be joined unto me, because I have born him three sons: therefore was his name called Levi. And she conceived again, and bare a son: and she said, now will I praise the LORD: therefore she called his name Judah."

—Genesis 29:33-35

Encouragement for Difficult Times

Being gracefully broken is a soft way to describe rejection, imperfection, and being mishandled at no fault of your own. Often, I have wondered why I haven't fit in or wasn't accepted. But I now know the reason is that no one can see my vision the way that God has given it to me, so they wouldn't have the same zeal or tenacity that I have to pursue it. I learned that I wasn't meant to fit in; I was meant to stand out. I encourage you that if you find yourself in similar positions, know that God's plans and purpose for your life expand further than where others can see you go. Many perceive others based on their past failures, present circumstances, or personal criteria, but you have to know whose you are, what you are and your "why". Walk by faith and not by sight; prayer is the key, and faith unlocks the door. You are fearfully and wonderfully made, and you are vitally fit for the Master's use. The challenges that have come to fertilize you are part of the process for birthing your vision. There is purpose for your pain, so I encourage you to behold the Son, have an ear to hear, be fitly joined, watch, pray and in everything, give God praise. Your reward is drawing nigh.

In this journey called life, things may not always go as we plan, that is why we should acknowledge God and put Him first. We must trust in Him to be our source, for nothing moves without the power of God. It is vital that we obtain wisdom for it is the principal thing; therefore, get wisdom, and with all thy getting get understanding. It is important that as women we know our worth, and that we do not go looking for love in the wrong places because it will only lead to disappointment. The Lord knows that I have had my share of disappointments. I was engaged three times which only led to heartache, and I was an unwed mother of four. The Word of God declares that whosoever findeth a wife findeth a good thing, and obtaineth favour of the Lord. A good friend shared with me on how everything she asked God for in a husband He granted her, so she was not only very wise in her request, but she had the faith that God would give her heart's desire. John 14:13-14 KJV says, "And whatsoever ye shall ask in my name, that will I do, that the Father may be glorified in the Son."

Leah's Fertile Years

As you read this chapter you will notice that Leah was not only a soft-eyed older daughter of Laban, and Rachel's older sister, but she was a woman of humility, strength, integrity, and faith. Leah was the first to give God praise. She is a matriarch and one of the four mothers of the 12 tribes of Judah. She endured rejection, hardship, torment, jealousy, mischief, bondage, and the reality of being both unloved and hated. But God rewarded her rejection by opening her womb and allowing her to bear the first offspring of Jacob and six sons. God perfected her in her weakness. Leah bore one daughter which was Jacob's seventh child and her situation ended like a love story.

Does one become unloved? Were they loved at some point and then suddenly hated? Leah prayed, "Surely the LORD hath looked upon my affliction now therefore my husband will love me." Leah desired for her husband Jacob to love her so badly that she called her broken heart an affliction, although it wasn't physical. It was emotional, mental, and spiritual and it is evident that she was being tormented night and day by the thought that her husband was in love with her younger sister Rachel. But the God of agape love, the love that has no conditions, He looked not on Leah's countenance and her outward appearance, but on her heart. He saw that she was hated and yet He honored her faithfulness and opened her womb.

"To everything there is a season and a time to every purpose under the heaven."   —*Ecclesiastes 3:1*

God blessed Leah to be fruitful and this period became her fertile years; she bore Jacob's first child and named him Reuben, which means son-offspring. She thought for sure after having his firstborn child, that Jacob would love her. In those times to give birth to a man's first male child was an honor. But the truth is that he was still in love with her sister Rachel.

It may seem as if Leah was trying to be a man pleaser, which is an impression of self-gratification, but that wasn't her intention at all. You see Leah's name means weary, but Jeremiah 1:5 declares, "Before I formed thee in the belly I knew thee, and before thou camest forth out of the womb I sanctified thee, and I ordained thee a prophet unto nations." I'm not saying that this scripture is referring to her being a prophet, but it is declaring the purpose in her life and that word still stands today. The point of the matter is that God knows our ending from our beginning. He sees everything that we face in life—the roads we take and even the choices we may have made that we are not proud of.

"Enter ye in at the strait gate: for wide is the gate and broad is the way, that leadeth to destruction, and many there be which go in there at."

—*Matthew 7:13-14*

God knows us and He cares for us. That is what is so great about serving Him. Because He is omniscient and omnipotent; He is infinite in power, therefore there is nothing too hard for Him. He has dunamis, which is Greek for power or ability. He is omnipresent, so when we make worship a lifestyle, we will have a perpetual encounter with Him because we are building a relationship. And although Leah seemed to become weary, she didn't deserve to be unloved. Everyone needs to be loved and she didn't ask to be in the position of Jacob's wife nor in a battle with her sister. Leah was unloved due to no fault of her own. Have you ever wondered, why me? Well, I am sure Leah did too; I know I have. When we find out what our God-given purpose is and walk in it, as unfolds, and you will understand that it is all a part of God's plan. So, if you haven't found out what your purpose is think about that very thing that you intend in your heart the most to do in pleasing God.

"That ye might walk worthy of the Lord unto all pleasing, being fruitful in every good work, and increasing in the knowledge of God."

—Colossians 1:10-14

You see Leah's process didn't start with Jacob, it started at the Garden of Eden. It didn't start in her father's house, her father decided to deceive Jacob by falsifying their business arrangement. Jacob originally sought after her sister Rachel, but their father delivered Leah to Jacob in the middle of the night. When Jacob arose the next morning, he was very disappointed, when he realized it was not who he expected. I can imagine his facial expression and how angry he was, and how humiliated Leah must have felt to be unadmired. Her husband was so disgusted by her presence; what a terrible way to be rejected after being given away.

"Fear thou not; for I am with thee be not dismayed; for I am thy God I will strengthen thee; yea I will help thee Yea I will uphold thee with the right hand of righteousness."

—Isaiah 41:10

Leah endured the drama with meekness and grace. Though tired, she sought the Lord with prayer and supplication, then in Genesis 29:33 she conceived again and bore another son and called his name Simeon, meaning hear, because the LORD hath heard that she was hated. "But there is therefore no condemnation to them which are in Christ Jesus who walk not after the flesh but after the spirit." Have you ever prayed for something for a long time and it seem like your prayers were going unanswered? Have you ever said, "why me?" or wished a certain thing didn't happen, or even wished it upon someone else?

"And he said, Hearken ye, all Judah, and ye inhabitants of Jerusalem, and thou king Jehoshaphat, thus saith the LORD unto you, Be not afraid nor dismayed by reason of this great multitude, for the battle is not yours, but God's."

—2 Chronicles 20:15

You see many people want the blessing but not the Blesser; they want the success without the test or going through the process. I heard a pastor say recently that God showed him how America is spoiled. The truth is anything that is worth having is worth fighting for, working for, and putting in the effort, but you have to choose your battles. Many of us are fighting battles that aren't even ours, and some battles we have already won. But like Rachel we have scales over our eyes and can't see clearly. God is just one prayer away and He will answer, but He works on His time not ours. The great thing about Him is that He is always on time.

Everything we do in life is based on the measure of faith that God has given every man. Yes, a man may say, you have faith, and I have works. Show me your faith without your works and I will show you my faith by my works. Without faith it is impossible to please Him, so we want to have the evidence of what we are asking Him for. We must activate our faith, stir it up, plant, work at it, believe it, and speak it so we can please Him. Then we will see the results. I often use a mustard seed as an illustration to describe faith because it is not in the size of the seed but what it produces. In Matthew 17:20 the Word of God declares, "If ye shall have faith as a grain of a mustard seed, ye shall say unto this mountain, remove hence to yonder place and it shall remove and nothing shall be impossible unto you."

Do you know that God is still in the womb-opening business? Yes, and He is still healing, today too! Let me share a portion of my HERstory with you. My oldest son was sick, and I was on the wall praying day and night. I questioned God as to why he wasn't being healed. I told the Lord that I had been faithful and I had prayed over other saints who were healed battling similar issues. I had even visited some I didn't know. Immediately, Matthew 17:21 came to me, "Howbeit this kind goeth not out but by prayer and fasting." When I went to respond the spirit of the Lord said fast and pray even more.

Out of obedience I began to do just that, aside from my daily Bible reading. I remember also investing in the book *Prayers that Rout Demons* by Apostle John Eckhardt. You see, God is intelligent and wise. I began to read this book to my son and had him repeat every word and scripture after me. In his distress he would often mess up the verse so I would have him repeat until he got it right and every time he did he would regurgitate. You may be wondering what this has to do with Leah and Jacob or how God compensates us for being rejected. Let me tell you. It is because God's Word shall not return to Him void, it accomplishes what it is sent to do. Believe me, I am going somewhere with this.

Rejection is real and it is a form of spurning a person's affections. It can change one's perspective of you, and push individuals into depression or oppression. My son was an outgoing, strong, healthy, handsome athlete and everyone loved him, especially all the young girls. He is the oldest grandson. My parents went to his games when I couldn't. When we moved into the city my other children and I had a lot of sleepless nights. We did have loving spiritual leaders and a few ministers that were of great influence. I thank God for those who were supportive during that time, although we went through a lot of rejection.

Because of that, one day changed my son's life. He was incarcerated, given medication in the city jail for months before being diagnosed and people's perception of him change drastically. I even lost a job because I had to assist in his care. The area in which we lived couldn't provide the proper care or therapy, so he was receiving virtual doctor's appointments. This was over ten years ago it and was hard for them to balance his medications to regulate the chemical imbalance he was experiencing. As a result, he began to have all types of side effects.

When a mother that is tired of being tired and begins to wail in the spirit for her family, for peace, for a breakthrough, for healing, and for an answer, she goes in violently. She makes commands to break chains, any spirit of restlessness, breaking legal rights of all generational spirits, asking God to cover, renouncing, denouncing, and destroying yokes and declaring and decreeing. Soon enough, what the devil meant for evil God will turn it around for your good, but your faith has to line up.

As I continued reading that book to him the doctors started asking questions. We were at the hospital and after blood work and tests they questioned what he had been eating. They said that whatever he swallowed had to be sharp. I assured them he didn't swallow anything, and I explained how one of his main side effects was that he barely had an appetite, and he had been regurgitating. Another nurse came in and said that for him to be as sick as he is, based on the CT scan reading, he looks pretty good. I said, "Praise God!" Nonetheless, they wanted to air lift my son because they said he had holes in his esophagus. His condition was so serious that he had to go right away and would have to have surgery immediately. They told me to go ahead to the next hospital because there was no room for me in the helicopter. I just nodded my head as I was praying in my spirit. Within 30 minutes the nurse came back and said Ms. Washington there are no helicopters in the area, so we will have to send him in an ambulance. You can ride along with him over there. While the EMT was prepping my son, I called in to my job because I was due to work that night. I explained the situation and the sirens began to go off.

As we arrived the surgeon and specialist approached. They asked if I knew what it was that my son swallowed. They said that he is a young man and if they performed the surgery, they would have to remove his chest cavity. If did that he had a 90 percent chance of not surviving. They said that before proceeding they would do their own testing and decide from there. Again, I assured them he didn't swallow anything. After they left, I made some calls and prayed on the phone with a few faith believers touching and agreeing for his healing, and that God would intervene on his behalf.

"For the LORD shall be thy confidence and shall keep they foot from being taken. Withhold not good from them to whom it is due. When it is in the power of thine hand to do it."

—Proverbs 3:26-27

As I walked back to area where my son was the Lord spoke to me and said, *wash his feet.* I asked the nurse for a basin, hot water and a towel and I had blessing oil. I began to pray in the spirit and as I was washing my son's feet the radiology team came to take him down for testing. I continued praying, quickly dried his feet and anointed him, hallelujah! I never got upset or shed a tear because I trusted the report of the Lord. He went down for testing and when he came back the doctor rolled the monitor over to me. Looking astonished, he told me that he didn't know what they'd seen at the other hospital, but he didn't see any holes my son's esophagus. He said there will not be any surgery, but they would keep him for observation. Given they were concerned that he may have swallowed something sharp, they decided to place him on suicide watch with a sitter in the room. I said okay and thanked him; I told him that and I would be staying as well. After that, I asked every sitter, doctor, nurse, housekeeper, and lab technician that came into his room, if I could I anoint them before they tended to him. They all allowed me to.

The Word of God declares in James 5:14, "Is any sick among you? Let him call for the elders of the church, and let them pray over him, anointing him with oil in the name of the Lord." Thank You Father! When you know your redeemer lives, when you know, there is no question in your mind if there's anything too hard for God. The Lord brought back to my remembrance that while the surgeons were trying to figure it all out that He had already worked it out. Don't you know there is wonder-working power in the blood of the Lamb? God gave me a revelation that it was spiritual thing— it was not natural. As it is written in Hebrews 4:12, "For the word of God is quick, and powerful, and sharper than any two-edged sword, piercing even to the dividing asunder of the soul and spirit, and of the joints and marrow, and is a discerner of the thoughts and intents of the heart."

Reflection

The Word of God is sharp, piercing. As I spoke and fed the Word into my son's spirit it cut. When he spoke it back fluently, he proclaimed it! The surgeons were thinking about removing his chest cavity, dividing joints and marrow, stating the rare chance of survival. I didn't receive it! I trusted God, I walked by faith, and I trusted Him. The compensation for rejection is miracles, signs, wisdom, wealth, and wonders.

"For the Lord shall be thy confidence, and shall keep thy foot from being taken."

—Proverbs 3:26

As we get back into Genesis 29:34, we see where Leah again conceives and bears a third son and names him Levi, which means attach or join, where she then questions God if her husband will be joined unto her now that she gave him three children. She figures she gave him not one, or two, but three, and her sister Rachel was barren. It must have been hard to go about their daily lives seeing each other at mealtime, or seeing Jacob go to the room of the other sister in the same house. During that time the culture justified this behavior. She asked God is Jacob going to be connected eye-to-eye, hip-to-hip, and be with her. Would she be the queen of his castle?

I recognized that during Jacob's journey, he acknowledges that every stone he sat as his pillar would be the house of God. So it wasn't that Jacob was a mean stubborn man who wanted to take women for granted, but he did desire a certain woman. He ended up with someone else and whom he didn't desire. Leah's rejection lingered on for so long that in reading this chapter some women might become upset or question why. I want to encourage any of you who are in relationships, engaged, or married to learn how to trust. Please don't give your sanity, joy, and happiness away to anyone. It is a form of bondage. Free yourself and give your troubles over to God.

For those of you who may be going through a "Leah experience" of rejection, of feeling left out or singled out, I want you to know that God cares for you. You are not your pain or your past. You are unique, bought with a price, and fit for the Master's use. Being rejected does not dictate your future and although you may be tired, weary, and disgusted it is only a test. Without what you are going through, or have gone through, you would not have a testimony. So, keep the faith; and whatever you do don't you dare give up. The strength it takes to turn around and go back is the same strength it takes to keep on pressing toward the mark of the high calling which is Christ Jesus. Remember that everything that you have been going through has been a set up to bless you. What the devil meant for evil God, meant for your good, according to His good pleasure. Be encouraged and know that if God be for you, it doesn't matter if the whole world is against you. His thoughts towards you are of peace and not evil and to give you an expected end. You shall win!

"But thanks be to God, which giveth us the victory through our Lord Jesus Christ."

—1 Corinthians 15:57

I believe that it was necessary for Leah to experience what she did. If you know Leah's history, you know that at first, she was also infertile and couldn't bear children. But God opened her womb, counted her faithfulness for righteousness, and turned her weariness into praise. When God saw she was hated, by her husband and sister, He looked at her heart, her worship, her prayer life, her supplication, and her humility. He honored her faithfulness and gave her gift after gift. Although she expected her husband to love her, she also knew God in a special way, and He gave her something to love her back and a way for her to feel needed.

Years ago, I knew a couple that adopted a child after years trying to conceive. The doctors told them that they couldn't have kids; but God had the final say. They ended up having their own child. A few years after adopting their daughter they had a son of their very own. Yes! He's able. My hope is built on nothing less, than Jesus' blood and righteousness! Do you have hope today? Well, Leah conceived again and bore a son. She said, Now, will I praise the LORD, and his name is Judah, which means praise. He was Jacob's fourth eldest son; the number four is a sign of spiritual wholeness, balance, and stability.

During her fertile years, Leah was chosen by God—not by Jacob. Many are called but few are chosen. Even the names that Leah chose to give her sons were significant, and a demonstration of her faithfulness to God, and her vows to Jacob although she had to share him. She was a woman of strength, and she had beauty within, she had poise and character. Her relationship with God had to be divine because His hands were upon her life even, in her distress. Leah and Jacob's love story goes far beyond the Bible's pages because she gave him something Rachel never could. She gave him the honor of his first child. The compensation for Leah's rejection was the fruit of her womb.

"Lo, Children are an heritage from the LORD, and the fruit of the womb is His reward."

—Psalms 127:3

In times like these, we soon learn to appreciate, love, give, share, embrace, celebrate, and rejoice at having the opportunity to create unique life-giving moments. What I can say is that tomorrow has its own ending, but today is mine. It is symbolic of unity and respect beyond what the world can offer. In actuality, we gain more than we ever could have lost because what we shared will always be a part of the memories that are held dear and near in the heart.

The Sisters' Big Rivalry: Rachel's Jealousy of Leah
(Genesis 30:1-2;6-8; 14-21)
Sharyn K. Dyer, BA, MPH

Sharyn's HERstory

Sharyn Dyer was born in the cool hills of Mandeville, Manchester Jamaica and now lives in Chicago. The miles between these spaces are symbolic of her many worlds colliding, leading her to discover recurring beauty, rebirthing, and grace. She received her Bachelor of Arts degree in Biology and her Master's in Public Health from the University of Illinois at Chicago where she serves as an instructor and seasoned administrator. Recently, Sharyn was appointed as an adjunct lecturer at the department level by the university; her appointment is currently pending approval by the campus.

When they are not doing "all of the things" that come with raising three, amazing human beings and their three little guinea pigs, Sharyn and her husband serve in outreach ministry through their historic church, Vernon Park Church of God, and around their local community.

A true artist at heart, Sharyn feeds her drive to create by reimagining things, spaces, and time. When she is not painting, gardening,

trying to recreate another dish without a recipe, or going through her laundry list of home projects, she gets lost in one of her favorite past times—thrifting. She also enjoys working with her ChiGraceDesigns.com clients to help them live where they love and love where they live.

This is her first Rich Gurlz Club Inc. book collaboration and she feels blessed to have had the opportunity to dive deeper into God's Word through the lens of a woman who was already worthy but had to discover that in her own time.

Chapter 8
The Sisters' Big Rivalry: Rachel's Jealousy of Leah
(Genesis 30:1-2;6-8; 14-21)
Sharyn K. Dyer

"When Rachel saw that she was not bearing Jacob any children, she became jealous of her sister. So she said to Jacob, "Give me children, or I'll die!" Jacob became angry with her and said, "Am I in the place of God, who has kept you from having children?"

—Genesis 30:1-2

I once heard that jealousy is worse than the grave, a place that is never satisfied. I wouldn't have known this to be true had I not experienced it. In the span of a decade, life brought some of the greatest tests that I can now gracefully accept as being a part of my life course. I can't recount it all here, but I am so grateful I can finally lift the words from my heart without bleeding. The jaws of jealousy have the power to crush those who find themselves under its weight. Proverbs 27:4 says it best, "Anger is cruel and wrath overwhelming but who can stand before jealousy."

The roots of jealousy, bitterness, envy, unforgiveness, and strife run deep and are destructive enough to complicate the most distant of relationships. So how much more can the ones nearest to you be affected? These issues often stretch back to the womb—the starting point—before we are thrust into the acculturation of life. These are the places where we begin to receive mixed signals about who we are, or that we are less than who we were created to be, less than enough. It is from the abyss of scarcity that the arms of jealousy reach for whatever they desire.

These same roots extend beyond Jacob's own birth story and pull him center stage into a dramatic rivalry. Afraid to deal with the repercussions of tricking his brother Esau out of his birthright, he tries to escape reality by running as far away as possible. But in a strange plot twist, while he thinks he is evading his past, he is instead pulled into a tug of war between his sister-wives. We usually expect to find such radical shifts towards the middle or end of an epic tale, but for Jacob this marks

the beginning of a reckoning with his own sibling rivalry. He fought to pull his brother back so he could cross the proverbial finish line first.

Not much is known about Leah and Rachel's childhood except for their birth order, and shallow hints about their physiques and emotional and spiritual maturity. I imagine that Rachel, being close in age to her older sister, grew accustomed to managing the simultaneous envy of all the countryside girls, and the doting attraction of the men in her life. Longing to trade a day in her sister's beauty, Leah probably had to deal with the constant angst of living in her younger sister's shadow, of being betrothed to the "better" twin brother. The simplicity of holding a conversation with a stranger was likely painful at best. Nonetheless, she had to work past her insecurities if she was to convince a suitor to fulfill her father's and grandfather Abraham's legacy of many nations.

What we do know is that as wives, it was a race to the finish line. Rachel had an excruciating time watching her slightly older sister become the first to bear children for a man whose eyes and affection were always only for her. Her jealousy was so great that she equated her inability to have children with death! One sister cherished. The other rejected. Both caught in a twisted web, existing in an identity outside of their own. Wasn't it enough that Leah was pawned off in the middle of the night only to have her dream of finally being loved aborted the next morning? Rachel's jealousy was inflamed seeing her sister bear not one but four sons for Jacob. Was she also to bear the burden of being rejected and carry the guilt of having more children than her sister?

Still reeling in the aftermath of not being first, Rachel's inner turmoil begins to show as she unravels publicly. Unable to control herself, she allows external happenings to send her into a whirlwind of blunders. Willing to do anything to feel like she was winning again, she demands that her husband do what only God can. Jacob bears the brunt of her misery and the impossible burden of correcting a biological limitation for which he only had the partial means to fulfill. He had zero control over what Rachel's womb could do. Yet, Rachel demanded he fix it right away.

Can you relate? Have you ever found yourself being blamed for someone else's unhappiness? If so, I am so sorry for whatever responsibility you were forced to assume. Perhaps you've tried to find the

solutions to your problems through dead ends?   May Rachel be a reminder to us all. Let us be careful to not lift our eyes more for affirmation or dependence on man than to God. If we believe that God is a man of His word, then we must also believe that our satisfaction, protection, and ultimately vindication can only come from Him.

My Genesis
For years, I was numb by the loss of my first baby sister. It occurred at a pivotal time in our lives. We were wives and mothers. We were also simply island girls now grown up and trying to find our way as women, in what still felt like a foreign land. Looking back, I was desperate for connection and in search of belonging. This made me extremely trusting of anything and anyone with the ability to breathe or make me feel at home.

Home was always offshore, a fruitful land nestled in the hills of Jamaica. My hometown sat in its cool central crests, elevated above sea level, where I watched those closest to me maneuver life's ebbs and flows through the building of relationships. Through my childhood eyes, we lived, worked, learned, played, and worshiped in a harmonious cadence that as an adult I still reach back for. These deep connections built on shared experiences seemed so easy to establish then. And while it was imperfect in many ways, it will always be home.

The stark realization of digging up roots at the age of sixteen and moving to a new country was both daunting and exciting. I was confident my childhood friendships would sustain me until I found my new tribe. And that they did. For the first several months, I would rush home from school, fling open the back door in search of a new stamp-laden envelope enclosed with freshly minted, double-sided, inked pages detailing all the things I'd missed in the last week. They were reminders of just how much I was missed.

There were updates on the couples who were still going steady or had broken up, holiday plans, Friday night youth group, and week-long conventions. These were the pages invisibly lined with our childhood memories bordered by margins filled with our history. The latest ones imprinting our minds were the late nights spent studying for our CXC exams. Those tests would mark the first chapter of our post-secondary lives. Our study nights often ended with all four of us piled on my mother's chartreuse-colored settee. It sat in our drawing room facing the big picture window overlooking our neighbor's expansive Ortanique Orange Grove. Not wanting to be apart from each other, we held on

tightly to those final moments in the weeks leading up to my departure. For good. Those were my sisters. No matter what, we would always be there for each other.

Life, however, eventually came between us and we struggled to keep in touch. The months became years and eventually those years turned into decades of space and time. Now wives and mothers, we hop on the occasional video call or react to one of many milestones on social media. All this in an effort to remain connected. In our endless march of life, we've come face to face with joys and triumphs, deep loss, and grief. To fill in those spaces would require an eternity of letters and several rounds of star-lit, evening chats, to fully unpack.

My new friendships in the States were effortless and comfortable. Many of them I still cherish. Soon, I began to settle into my new church, school and eventually work. But perhaps it was my intimate understanding of what having to start again really meant, an innate need to belong, that drove me into relationships. I was always looking for deep connection particularly after my sister passed away. Not that this longing was unhealthy, but I realized in those early years, there was a deficit in me that led me to seek human approval in return for validation and a sense of worth.

As friendships and relationships evolved, I became familiar with the horrible feeling of being a pawn in someone else's corporate game. I felt the recurring trauma of allowing myself to be the receptacle for someone else's noxious venom. I have been labeled sensitive and had my personal experiences invalidated by the taut reality of others. I endured the unfortunate sting of rejection time and again because of my unhealthy expectation to be loved by those who simply didn't have, nor desired, the capacity to do so. There was also the guilt of creating healthy boundaries that were helpful to me, but were, in turn, hurtful to others. I was no longer able to move past these events as just another test. So, I finally decided to do the hard work of unpacking the cumulative events that tried to distort my view of who I was. The rejection wasn't just correction. It was elevation, in my understanding that in God's

119

eyes, I was altogether beautiful and worthy.

Then Rachel said, "God has vindicated me; he has listened to my plea and given me a son." Because of this, she named him Dan. Rachel's servant Bilhah conceived again and bore Jacob a second son. Then

Rachel said, "I have had a great struggle with my sister, and I have won." So she named him Naphtali.

—Genesis 30: 6-8

What an odd position to take, winning by whatever means necessary. It is a dog-eat-dog world, except these were sisters going at it. Sister-hate at its best. For Rachel, winning was an affirmation that she was ahead of her opponent. Like Rachel, if we are not completely secure in our position in God, we can easily end up taking on or projecting pain to those around us. We end up hanging jealousy and shame on others in the name of winning.

A while ago, an older friend gifted me a beautiful gold necklace with an odd-looking pendant. There was something superstitious about it, but I couldn't put my finger on it. The gift's source made it somewhat sentimental, so I decided to keep it with the intentions of exchanging it for something else later. So many good things were happening around me at the time, and I was excited to share my positive news with those close to me. What I hadn't anticipated was that while I was celebrating the unfolding of fulfilled promises, there would be folks who were in my circle but not my corner. I was unwittingly caught in the middle of someone else's competition. It was all or nothing. A masterful web of deceit. It was a relentless game of scoring a rubicon against the opponent. The only way to settle the score is by adding the loser's points to theirs.

I scoured the internet to try to learn more about the necklace I'd received. Apparently, it was part of a gift-giving practice that dated back to the second century. At the end of the necklace's delicate gold links was an evil eye charm meant to ward off bad luck. Wearing the necklace meant I would be guarded against another person's envy or malicious attempts. It is believed this was the same evil eye Sarah cast on Hagar before sending her away. Somehow, this dear friend of mine recognized the jealousy at play from others. She was trying to do everything she knew to do to protect me.

Of the strange occurrences in that season of my life, that one was by far the most memorable. Waking up to my husband praying over me early one morning solidified the fact that I was in a battle. It was spiritual and I needed to fight this one differently. I needed to wrestle this one with worship. I had to learn whatever it was I needed to know through this test so I wouldn't have to take it again. I had to decide to not let others' perceived winning take me off course. I had to choose to unhook my self-worth from performing for other people's opinions.

Don't be upset when the ones who hurt you seemingly carry on with their lives, unbothered by how it affected you. When it seems as though they are winning, remember that God is always fighting for you. You don't have to jump into a competition that was not designed for you. You don't have to raise the ante as a means of remaining relevant to others. Leah had the right to say no to Rachel but for whatever reason, she jumped back in the race. If we are not careful, and if we allow others' views of who we are to guide us, we will find ourselves headed down a slippery slope of people pleasing. Like comparison, it is a never-ending cycle of jumping through one hoop to the next to try to prove your love or commitment. Whether you feel like you are in first or last place, God's promises for you are sure. His method and timing for fulling your promises are secure.

"During wheat harvest, Reuben went out into the fields and found some mandrake plants, which he brought to his mother Leah. Rachel said to Leah, "Please give me some of your son's mandrakes." But she said to her, "Wasn't it enough that you took away my husband? Will you take my son's mandrakes too?" "Very well," Rachel said, "he can sleep with you tonight in return for your son's mandrakes."

—Genesis 30:14-15

Have you ever found yourself caught up in someone else's drama wondering how you missed the opportunity to decline the invitation? Those are the events you discover on your calendar that you didn't schedule. On a good day, they are one-and-done drive-bys. Other times, the episodes shamelessly hop from one life season to the next. No matter how much you try to cancel the invite, or prepare for the unsuspecting pop-up, it appears when you least expect it—without even the courtesy of a reminder.

Picture this. Leah is in her tent apartment on a lovely Spring wheat harvest day while doing her best to maintain some peace on her side of the fields. She looks up to see Rachel beep-bopping her way about to make demands on her day. Desperate to have a child of her own, Rachel's jealousy morphs itself into a demand for something she is not even entitled to. In her mind, she is convinced she deserves it. She makes a brazen request for her sister's prized mandrake plants. And to add insult to injury, she offers absolutely nothing in return!

There was not even a friendly "Hello! How are the kids?" No offer for a play date or consideration that her sister might be exhausted from all the things that go with caring for a gaggle of children. I have three and so I know! It is not until Leah confronts her sister's audacity and defends her place in the first wives' club that Rachel concedes. The squabble ends with a paltry exchange for a night with Jacob.

Now, what is interesting about this incident is that the mandrake plant is known in certain regions of the world as an aphrodisiac and as a symbol of fertility. If the mandrake fruit extract were to ever grace the shelves of your nearest department store, it would likely be bottled in the shape of a sweet, little love apple. All parts of the plant have been said to carry hallucinogenic properties—from the stalkless leaves that shoot directly from the tuberous roots to the yellow-green or bluish-purple colored flowers that bear the yellow fruit. I would like to think Rachel desired the plants for any one of the properties mentioned. But the main thing to recognize about jealousy is that its appetite will never be satisfied. Jealousy says, "I want to replace [insert person/place/thing] with [me/myself/I]." Rachel coveted her sister's mandrake plants simply out of her obsessive need to win. Leah was now ahead of the game with four sons while Rachel was yet to have one of her own. She never knew what it was like to feel inferior to her sister and she couldn't handle it.

Previously, Rachel's device of choice was her maidservant Bilhah. Today it was her sister's mandrakes. Tomorrow it would be something else. Her memory falls short again and she forgets to consider the rejection her sister experienced. Failing to see the opportunity to participate in her sister's happiness by loving on her beautiful nephews, Rachel remains in a self-absorbed state. She failed to find within her the courage to manage her emotions and see her sister's children as a direct connection to the promise. Instead, she chose to elevate the children of her maidservant for the sake of being in the running to become first.

What kind of sisterhood is this? With this kind of toxic dynamic, it's no wonder that Leah seemed guarded in protecting her son's mandrakes. The pain was still palpable. I have no evidence from the following statement, but it wouldn't seem farfetched to think that maybe, just maybe, it occurred to Leah that the mandrakes would momentarily alter her feelings of abandonment and her perceptions of an unloved reality, not just from Jacob but from another woman, her blood sister.

You might be faced with a situation that is very annoying or confusing. Maybe you are getting mixed signals from people who are supposed to love you or respect your boundaries. They are supposed to be considerate and have your best interest at heart. At all costs, don't allow the external noise to take root inside. That noise is sometimes much louder than the confusing situations around us. And if we are not careful, we might start to believe the false alarms. Recognize the noise, focus on praise, and ask Holy Spirit to help you in your response.

"So, when Jacob came in from the fields that evening, Leah went out to meet him. "You must sleep with me," she said. "I have hired you with my son's mandrakes." So he slept with her that night."

—*Genesis 30: 16-17*

We are all yearning for something. Even with several children between them, the hunger for that "one thing" remained insatiable. Could they ever be satisfied? When would it be enough? Along the way, Leah somehow lost the peace she discovered after Judah's birth. How could she declare "This time I will praise the Lord" in one season and then, "You must sleep with me" in the next? The culling tentacles of jealousy sucked her into a comparison trap that left her feeling inferior to her sister again. Comparison will always show up as the masked bandit of joy. This is the inner critic that says, "You are not worthy of

123

that. Not pretty enough, not lovable. Too needy." Comparison will suck you back into competition by parading how they one-upped you.

When you compare yourself to others, you come up short every single time. For this one reason, we are cautioned to guard our hearts. From the heart flows the issues of life. From the abundance of the heart, the mouth unearths our deepest thoughts. While you cannot control the actions of others, you can control what you choose to focus on. You are in control of your perspective on the matters of life. You and only you can control the thermostat of what you are feeling. You have the power to determine how you respond.

You have probably heard it before. Your thoughts are fertile. What you feed is what grows. What you meditate on is what manifests. I recently came across a new iteration of the serenity prayer that opened my eyes to see that peace is accepting the people I cannot change. It is finding the courage to change the only person I can. Wisdom is knowing that that person is me!

Lord grant me the serenity to accept the people I cannot change,
the courage to change the one I can
and the wisdom to know it is me.

—*Unknown*

Please hear me when I say that forgiveness is not giving those who hurt you permission to hurt you again. Instead, it gives you permission to be set free to the point where you are no longer a prisoner to the pain. In her journey to move on and make peace with her painful past, the author, Lysa Terkeurst, affirmed that forgiveness is both a decision and a process. Just because you decide to forgive, doesn't mean your heart, body and mind will automatically sync with your journey. There are times you might question your commitment. The signs of physiological betrayal might leave you questioning your resolve. Did I truly forgive? Is God pleased with my forgiveness plan? There might also be the temptation to accelerate spiritual performances hoping to remind yourself that you are still good, and you didn't deserve this.

In your attempts to make sense of your experiences, know that the process of forgiveness is iterative. Your human frailties have already been accounted for. There is a reason God asks us to take up our cross. That is because he promised to do the hard part and carry our issues. We just need to learn to give our cares over to him. Not once but daily. He is big enough to cover the shame of what happened to you. Choosing to deal with the impact of the trauma takes time but don't allow the frustrations of the process delay the transformative healing you deserve. So, grace yourself and start the journey of forgiveness today. No matter how imperfect it might feel.

"God listened to Leah, and she became pregnant and bore Jacob a fifth son. Then Leah said, "God has rewarded me for giving my servant to my husband." So, she named him Issachar." —Genesis 30: 17-18

The Scriptures don't provide details of Leah's prayers, but God listened to her each time. It might have been the pure posture of Leah's heart that allowed God to continually turn a tender ear to her voice. She wasn't perfect but having experienced God's peace in her life before, she knew who her source was. Even when she strayed, she knew how to find her way back. Through a feud over mandrake plants, God searches the topography of their hearts to see where their dependence was. He didn't have to dig too deeply to realize that Leah's heart posture pleased him. And so, yet again, he blesses her with another son.

What is interesting is that there was always room at the table for both women. They both had the prize but got hung up on the process of when, how and how much of it they received. Each of their paths were different. God listened to Leah in her fruitful years and remembered Rachel in her barren ones. That is what the mercy of God looks like. What was different was His timing and how He chose to bless them. Their struggles uniquely shaped their desperate realities and God knew this. His provision for them was ordered by a tailor-made kind of grace. How God chooses to lead us to our destination is not duplicative. It's prescriptive. His design for your life and purpose is unique to you and only you. It won't look like anyone else's.

There were moments in my own life where I questioned what felt like a failure on God's part to protect me. The satisfaction of surviving and keeping on ticking when I got a licking became less and less appealing. I no longer regarded it as some badge of honor for my physical or spiritual strength. The truth is, God isn't blind to the tenuous situations we find ourselves in. He is not blind to our unfair circumstances, and He certainly isn't unaware of the vehicles that transported us there.

Even in her momentary weakness, God demonstrates to Leah that provision can only come from Him. Rachel may have bartered for mandrakes, but Leah is the one who ended up with the promise of another child. Once again, God proves himself to be her only source of contentment. As He did for Leah, my prayer is that you, too, will know that He sees you and yearns to listen to you. He will always act on behalf of His children. He will always pursue the matters of your heart. He will always be your God and your very great reward.

"Leah conceived again and bore Jacob a sixth son. Then Leah said, "God has presented me with a precious gift. This time my husband will treat me with honor, because I have borne him six sons." So she named him Zebulun. Some time later she gave birth to a daughter and named her Dinah."

—Genesis 30:21

After all these years seeking affirmation, it must have been hard for Leah not to think of God as unkind. The tears somehow found their way. Her eyes were not only weak in beauty but weak from endless crying. As life transitioned, she marked the chapters through the naming of her children. Their names carried the unbelievable memories of her life unfolding. The questions created a mountain of shame, rejection, disappointment, and anger. How did I find myself here again? I am certain by now I should have gotten this right. How could I be so foolish, so trusting, so desperate? Why did God allow this divide between my sister and me? Why didn't He protect me? The questions must have been mentally draining.

Your life courses are not always chosen. Sometimes they choose you. Know that none of your experiences will be wasted. Jesus was willing to endure all of this and more when he gave his life. Distractions are inevitable but what if he allowed the distraction to take him off course? Where would we be?

Maybe you have marked a transition in your life by an unplanned life event, a deferred or dissolved dream or the sting of rejection or loss. Know that you are not a victim of your circumstance. So, affirm God's love for you not just in your thoughts but in your confession. In those major transitions in life, find a way to give God glory. Tell your story of how you overcame. Recall His goodness and how He brought you out of your dark nights. Whatever you do, find a way to extract your story from the pages of you heart.

Some time later, Leah had a daughter Dinah, whose name means vindicated. The temptation to want to tell your side of the story or to seek revenge is part of the human experience. You may never receive the apology you've held your breath for. It might continue to look as though God's blessing on their lives is a nod of approval for their bad behavior towards you. But keep your eyes fixed on the things that are true. Sometimes there is room for reconciliation and other times there is not. Vindication isn't always revenge or seeing the ones you hurt you, hurt in return. Sometimes vindication is simply reconciling what the distortions of life might lead you to believe about yourself and what God says to be true.

This mystifying thing called relationships will always stretch every part of who you are. For better or for worse, we all bear within us a history connected to us in the womb. When we enter any relationship, we open ourselves up to the variety of their roots. Please don't be surprised by them. Not even yours. Even Jesus had a Judas in his circle. So be mindful of who you allow into your corner. Guard your heart so you are secure in who God says you are. These things will help you in your response to them. Are you ready to trust Him as your defender? The One who brings you honor? Your vindicator? Your very great reward?

My Exodus

It was time. Time to confront the source of the numbing. I welcomed the brokenness. Ready to unlock the words that felt choked up in my throat, that for years only allowed me to listen. I was face-to-face with the unhealthy thoughts about who I was, as I embarked on my journey to healing. All the while, Abba's love was right there. It tenderly washed over me, pulling me closer to the safe bounds of His bosom.

Forgiving those who let me down was hard. Finding the grace to forgive myself for not loving myself enough was even harder. As the memories ebbed and flowed in and out of my mind, it took everything in me to cling to what felt like cliché promises; somehow it was for my good. Somehow my joy would come in the morning.

No matter how much it seemed those who hurt me won, He assured me over and over again, that my portion was secure. What He had stored up for me wasn't anyone's to take. You are not the sum total of someone else's game score. You are not the score of their opinions. God's truth will always ground you as an anchor and guide you as a compass. After years of listening, I finally heard His answers. I was already loved. I was already enough. I was already worthy.

References:

Bible Hub: https://biblehub.com/commentaries/genesis/30-1.htm

Britannica: https://www.britannica.com/plant/mandrake-Mandragora-genus

Jewish Women's Archive: https://jwa.org/encyclopedia/article/leah-midrash-and-aggadah

Jewish Virtual Library: https://www.jewishvirtuallibrary.org/leah

Mathew Henry Commentary:

https://www.biblegateway.com/resources/matthew-henry/Gen.30.1-Gen.30.13

https://www.biblegateway.com/resources/matthew-henry/Gen.30.14-Gen.30.24

Terkeurst, L., *Forgiving What You Can't Forget: Discover How to Move On, Make Peace with Painful Memories And Create a Life that is Beautiful Again.*

Laughing on the outside and crying on the inside. I can tell you about falling apart in the presence of others and they don't have a clue.

You see, they fail to recognize that loving my man seems to hurt me more than it does him. Before you judge me, by saying this is just another woman's tale of "hating on men," let me assure you that I love men more than I could ever hurt them.

Sisters know what I mean when I say I want to scream while I'm sharing my coveted dream of success. They know that fame and prosperity does not necessarily mean happiness and joy from all who truly know you. They can tell you about the value of "Casting your bread upon the waters," and that one day you will look up and there is a deposit into your self-esteem account. Sisters endorse you, appreciate you, and support you without a withdrawal financially and emotionally. With them, you can expect more from life's ever-increasing abundance. Many people will give you genuine respect and gratitude for the service that you provide, but how sad, when the man in your life resents the success and accolades that you receive from others.

A lot of people could care less about your greatness, your power, prestige, and faith. All they care about is what you can do for them. You are a signature design that allows few people to experience the favor of your love and savor of your company. Your pain is almost palpable and the hurt too deep to comprehend. The brother you are aligned with does not value your exquisite persona or your versatility that reaches beyond your circumstances to embrace your style and creativity. It hurts to know that you are never good enough, never smart enough, never pretty enough, never affluent enough, never "street" enough to be on the level of acceptance that will keep him by your side. But hold on. The best is yet to come. Forget that hogwash about you not being up to his standards. What standards are those?

Sister, you are incredible and free to be all you can be. The brother cannot deal with you because he can see potential and greatness in you that others may simply dream of. He knows there is a natural grace to you that is long lasting and not a fleeting moment to trifle with. Understand, that when a man can claim your mind, he can claim your spirit, as well as your body. Pain can easily become your bedfellow and hurt your relationships as depression envelope your soul. You are a strong woman of faith. Let the tears come for they are a refreshing fountain, although you cannot stay at the well continually. Allow the love of God to rejuvenate and restore you into the rightful place where you belong: a place of harmony and balance. Show yourself some love and you will discover that no man will ever love you as the Creator can.

You are a trendsetter, bold and beautiful, with an identity of your own. You must never allow anyone to define who you are as a person or a woman. Be inspired by women of the past and their stories, of pain and heartache that often tore the frame and foundation from under their careers. Keep reading until you see where these women finally discovered the word "me." A lot of people talk about greatness, but they settle for mediocrity. Many of us have been there and stayed long enough to discover that we never want to re-live the experience again. We don't have to compete with the man in our life, and if you have to, you need to run for your life. Maximize whatever time you have to change the circumstances surrounding you because your health and wellness may depend on it.

This is your time to be proactive in erasing years of crying over old wounds and devastating scars that won't go away. While still visible, but they lose their sting and their power when you learn to let go. Do not allow a man to dictate who you are in life and how high or low you can go. If he loves you, he will encourage and support you, no matter what. To him, it is about the "we" and not the put-downs or the "less than." It is up to you to transform your life choices into a compassionate and confident investment in your future.

Be the same person regardless of your title, your family, your job, religious denomination or beliefs, your relationships, your financial status, and your fame or lack of. Predict success, expect success, and receive what you say you can have, because the promise is yours.

Chapter 9

Jacob: A Pawn in Women's Love Games
(Genesis 30: 3-5; 9-21)
Sheila Dudley

Sheila's HERstory

I've lived in Chicago, IL all my life. I grew up in the Robert Taylor homes with eight siblings, have five half-brothers and one half-sister. I had my first child when I was 20 years old. We moved out a year and a half later in 1986. I now have three children—all young adults ages 37, 32, and 27. My mom passed away when I was very young. My dad took care of us the best he knew how. My grandmother on my mom's side wanted to take us in. I remember my dad saying no, that he would raise us. I thank him for keeping us all together, though growing up in the "PJs" (projects) was rough. There was a lot of gun violence, gangs, shootings, rape, family fights, theft, and sexual immorality. Negativity in my environment was the norm.

I graduated from William Dubois Point Dusable in 1982 with a scholarship to Columbia College for Music and Arts. I started playing flute in the third grade and continued throughout high school. Occasionally, I still play. I can play other instruments as well. I played in the marching band, concert band, and jazz band, and played with The

Barrett Brothers outside of school. I played for Orchestra Hall twice and won first and second place flute soloist. Instead of attending Columbia, I had a change of plans and attended Illinois School of Commerce.

I graduated from there with an Associate Degree in business economics.

While in high school I attended a Catholic church seeking the Lord. I went on their retreats. From there I attended three Baptist churches. I was baptized in name of the Father, Son and Holy Ghost twice. One day, a friend of mine from the world, whom I later married, invited me to his sister's church, Gateway Apostolic Faith Church in the PCAF. I visited again in 1992. In 1993 the Lord saved me and filled me with his precious Holy Ghost; that same year I was baptized in Jesus' name. I knew I was in the truth. I served and held several local, state, and national titles. I was called to the ministry in 1997, and I didn't start preaching until 1998. The Lord used me mightily as a street evangelist. He started me out that way first. My first message was on the bus on 55th and Cottage Grove "Repent for the kingdom of God is at hand." My first church message was called 'Be ye Holy for I am Holy". I also served on the Shiloh Temple Church telecast from 2010 to 2011. I was ordained as an evangelist in the Pentecostal of Assemblies of the World. I still hold a title as a Sunday school teacher and am a member of the Indiana Pentecostal Church of God, where the late Bishop Charles E. Davis was pastor. He passed away in February 2021.

I hold a B.A. in Biblical Studies and Bachelor of Science in management. Currently, I run the Not Forgotten Ministry that provides teaching and street evangelism.

Chapter 9
Jacob: A Pawn in Women's Love Games
(Genesis 30: 3-5; 9-21)
Sheila Dudley

In the thirtieth chapter of the book of Genesis verses 1-2, Rachel realizes she couldn't bear any children for her husband Jacob. She became very jealous of her sister and asked her husband to give her children, or she would die. Desperation had gripped her soul. Her mental state was unstable; she was deciding to die. Rachel was extremely impatient. She should've allowed God to deal with her and wait on Him.

Meanwhile, this made her husband Jacob furious. He asked her, "Am I in the place of God, who has kept you from having children?" In other words, I am not your maker, blame God. I can't do anything. In reading the scripture, I realized Rachel was so hard on herself in wanting children. Her emotions took complete control. She had suicidal thoughts. Her will was not lined up with the Word of God. She looked at others, instead of keeping her eyes on her Maker. Instead of trusting God she took upon herself to accuse her husband of not giving her children, and then asked him to lie down with her handmaid Bilhah to have children for her. Genesis 30:3 says, "So she said, 'Here is my maid Bilhah; go in to her, and she will bear a child on my knees, that I also may have children by her.'" The phrase "bear a child on my knees" is a form of surrogacy by insemination. Our biblical ancestors were familiar with the idea of "building families through surrogacy" (Shulamit, 2019). Sarah said the same thing to Abraham in Genesis 16:2-3. In Sarah's case, after the child was of age she became jealous of her handmaid and put her and the child out of the house. Surrogate mothers in Jewish history were known to be thrown out of the house. Surrogate non-Israelite women became part of Jewish history as the first culture to use surrogation. These practices were not uncommon.

Emotional Discontent

Jacob is a man who knew whom he loved the most. His emotions were shared with four women: his first wife, Leah, his second wife, Rachel, Rachel's handmaid Bilhah, and Leah's handmaid, Zilpah. If we were to examine Jacob's emotions, at some point we'd see that he was unstable in his feelings. Only one woman, Rachel, whom he served for fourteen years to marry, was the beautiful love of his life. Jacob only had

true feelings for her but was romantically involved with other women.

Jacob is known for his past as the deceiver who tricked his brother Esau out of his birthright and their father's blessing. Jacob was favored by their mother, who also was a deceiver—it was in the blood line as his uncle Laban was deceptive as well. Esau was favored by their father Isaac. Jacob experienced a moment of himself; deception was played on him by Rachel's father. Rachel was his good thing. But in their country, it was the law to marry the older daughter before the younger.

Sadly, his first wife Leah was unloved by Jacob. Leah was the wife who was unattractive. Leah's name in Hebrew means weary, and alternately related to a cow. Leah had weak eyes which made her to look unappealing to Jacob. Weak eyes are associated with a lack of physical attraction or delicate (Bible Hub, 2021). Imagine, or maybe it has happened to you, being married to someone who doesn't love you. Then imagine your spouse was tricked into the marriage. You live with this person every single day, knowing his heart is with another woman. Even in intimacy, who do you think Jacob thinking about when he's with Leah?

Jacob became discontent. He was caught in two sisters' rivalry. He was a pawn in women's love games. Dictionary.com defines the word pawn as a person serving as security, or a hostage. Jacob was a "love hostage". His love was secured for Rachel. Yet Leah's love for Jacob held him hostage because she gave him children first. Let me pause right here.

I remember, as a teenager a relative told me that no one would never want me. I can truly relate to Leah's feelings. That statement stayed in my mind for quite some time. When I was in high school there was a lot of dating going on. There was one young man who liked me and was interested in becoming my boyfriend. We dated on and off throughout my high school years. I truly believe it didn't work out because of the negative words spoken over me. I was so hard on myself. He would say very nice things to me, but I didn't believe it because of the bad thoughts that invaded my mind.

During prom season in my senior year, I really desired to go. There was a young man I liked and was attracted to. I told myself I wouldn't mind going on prom with him. But the first thing I heard was the voice that told me nobody would ever want me. My emotions drew up and I went into a shell. Since then, every time I saw him, I would hide

and didn't want him to see me. Thank God I have come into the knowledge of the truth in Jesus Christ and understanding of God's Word. Proverbs 18:21 says, "The tongue has the power of life and death, and those who love it will eat its fruit." Those words of death were operating in my life because I had chosen to believe what my relative spoke over me. I encourage you to never believe anything negative that people have to say about you. Remember, God holds your future, and you have a purpose.

It was getting close to prom, and I still had no date. All my high school friends were talking about their dates, the colors they were wearing, and how their parents were so happy to support them. I got angry because my prom should have been memorable, and I was about to miss it because I didn't have anyone to take me.

I reached out to the guy I was dating on and off. He mentioned that he was going to ask to take me on prom, but our relationship had ended before he had the chance. He told me he would get back to me and he did. Mind you, I wasn't saved during this time. The happier I got about going to prom, the more the negative emotions and thoughts were trying to overtake me. Now that I understand spiritual things, I know that the negative thoughts were caused by a spirit that was assigned to harass me and make me feel like I wasn't worth anything. I had to get my emotions together to make this prom date work. I was a wreck. Finally, he asked me to the prom. I was so glad, but the bad thoughts came again. I wrestled with them for weeks.

I remember telling myself, I would dress up every day to help me feel better about myself. I thought miniskirts, heels, jewelry, and makeup were going to do it. I know now that I was dressing up my flesh, just desiring to be wanted. I was young and didn't understand how and why I was feeling the way I was. Growing up without a mother I couldn't ask her why certain things are happening to me in my puberty years and after. So, I can understand Leah. She had no one to encourage her, just like I had no one to encourage me. I learned that when I dressed up going to school, I felt important, feminine, and self-confident. I didn't understand the idea of royalty back then, but that's how I felt—very important. I had to accept myself for who I was—not what a person said about me. King David said it like this in Psalm 139, "For thou hast possessed my reins: thou hast covered me in my mother's womb. I will praise thee; for I am fearfully and wonderfully made! Glory to God! Marvelous are thy works; and that my soul knoweth right well." Now I am confident in who I am because God said that I am fearfully and wonderfully made. He made everything beautiful in His time. I am one of His prized beauties.

Eventually the day of my prom came. Growing up in the projects many families of high schoolers were coming out looking sharp. Neighbors shouted praise for those of us who were attending prom and for our dates—what an exciting moment in my life! I was going to prom in a limousine, feeling beautiful and good about myself and my handsome date. My hair was put up in a French roll with lots of curls, and I wore the prettiest cream lace and chiffon dress with matching shoes and purse. It was a day to remember!

Prom was therapeutic. It began to heal me of feeling sorry for myself. When I got saved some years later, the Lord took me down memory lane. I began to start reversing the affects, of ill- spoken words people have said to me. If you have been told anything negative or degrading, begin to decree and declare what is true about you to reverse those word curses over your life. You will see the manifestation of healing and chains broken off your life. Healing and deliverance shall be your portion. Isaiah 10:27 says, "It shall come to pass in that day, that his burden shall be taken away from off they shoulder, and his yoke from off thy neck, and the yoke shall be destroyed because of the anointing."

Leah and the Five "U's"

I experienced these "u's" the way Leah did; she was unwanted, unloved, unhappy, undeserved, and unconsidered. Jacob did not consider Leah's love for him after she gave him six sons and a daughter. Leah was looking for love in all the wrong places and ways, thinking that giving children to man who didn't love her like he loved her sister, would change his feelings. I grew up living in the Robert Taylor Homes in Chicago, IL. My mother passed away from breast cancer when I was

11 years old. I didn't have anyone to teach me about relationships, love, abstinence, self-worth, who I was, or why I was alive. Back in those days just about every teenage girl had a boyfriend. Large families were on the rise. Young girls were promiscuous (we called it being "fast" back then), growing up before their time or participating in sexual immorality to be popular. Everyone knew "who had who". In 1983, a year out of high school, I worked in a program called the Mayor Jane Byrne Job Coalition. I met a young man who also worked in the program. He was attractive to me, but in my mind all I heard were those "words of torment" again. *No one will want me.* He was a handsome young man; he wanted to get to know me and start a relationship. My heart would always be racing because I didn't know much about relationships. I saw them happening around me but didn't know what I was getting into. From a young teenager, I felt unloved, unwanted, unhappy, undeserving, and unconsidered.

My dad was always working on the road to support me and my siblings. He wasn't around much. I thank God that he raised us the best way he knew how. The young man at work kept trying to convince me that he truly liked me. So, I dated him and in 1984 I had my first child. I didn't know how to mother a child. I still didn't know what real love was. I was unlearned in so many things. When I look back over my life of being in relationships—having babies out of wedlock—I believe, I had the same idea Leah and Rachel had. We were racing to have children thinking that was where real love would come from. Jacob was caught up as a "Pawn for Women's Love Games". It wasn't Jacob's fault he didn't love two women at the same time. He loved only one woman and was romantically involved with Leah and her handmaiden. How could one person love two people at the same time? Is it possible? I think it's impossible because that person doesn't have all of you. Our hearts are not built that way. People say, "yes you can," but God says you can't serve two masters. You will love one and hate the other. King Solomon loved strange women. I can't see him loving all 400 wives and 300 concubines the same. There had to be at least one he truly loved; don't you think? With the pregnancies I had, I was looking for the love of my babies' fathers. My children do not have the same father, unlike Leah and Rachel's children.

I had five pregnancies. Three children were born; I had one miscarriage and one abortion. I wasn't saved during this time. I didn't have guidance. All I knew was that I couldn't take care of another child.

I had moved in with my sister. I was not in a good place during those years. When I got saved, the devil tormented my thoughts with what I had done to my unborn baby. I was convicted about aborting a child. I informed my previous pastor, and she simply said that I was forgiven because I wasn't saved when I did it. What a relief to my conscience knowing that I was forgiven, because the devil had my mind full of blame, shame, and guilt. Romans 8:1 says, "There is therefore now no condemnation to them which are in Christ Jesus, who walk not after the flesh, but after the Spirit."

In retrospect God was calling me to Himself in the mid-eighties, to prevent all that I went through while looking for true love. God wanted to show me His love for me, instead of me going from one relationship to another having babies, giving myself to men without a commitment to marriage, trying to find love. I wanted their love and thought they would love me because I had their children. What a big slap in the face! I grew up searching for love and it was not in my household, it was not in my relationships, it was not in my friends and, truthfully speaking, it wasn't complete in marriage in the way I thought it should be. I only found true love in Jesus and have come to be happy and satisfied in Christ.

I wanted to be loved, desired, happy, deserving and considered. But I learned how the hard way. Let's look at love. What is true love? For one thing it's not a feeling. True love is what you do. The way God did. He loved us and sent His Son to die on the cross for us. Now that's love. His unconditional love. These are seven signs of love:

1. Caring unconditionally. There is no "condition" requiring you do something for me, and I will do something for you. The way God loves us is unconditional.

2. Acceptance. You will accept the person you are with just the way they are—flaws and everything because we are not perfect. You can't change a person. Only the Spirit of God can. I honestly believe Leah thought she could change Jacob's heart to love her because she bore his children. Any woman or young lady who thinks you can change a person by having their babies is sadly mistaken. This is not love or even close to it.

3. Conversational. There are no secrets. You can tell each other everything. You are open and completely truthful. You share your

138

thoughts with each other.

4. Be the real you. You are not pretending to be somebody you are not. This is called being authentic or genuine. He or she will love you even more if you are yourself.

5. Respect. You must listen to and give respect to hear each other's point of view. It's not just one ear listening and turning the other ear. You are striving to resolve any disagreements. You regard each other's point of view.

6. Values. Everyone's background is not the same; ethics and values are usually different. Most of the time one person's background attracts the other.

7. Happiness. I learned that in marriage you have to be happy with yourself. Happiness is totally different from joy. Your mate can buy you things, do things for you and it lasts temporarily, until the moment he or she makes you mad and upset. Then the good thing that person did for you goes out the window. You don't feel happy about what he or she did.

When two people have the spirit of God real joy comes with it. Love, peace, and joy are found in Jesus. In relationships you are supposed to come together to grow even stronger. I'm going to add one more to the list.

8. It takes work. Relationships in marriage are based on teamwork. That's commitment and partnership. This will bring satisfaction because you both are working together. It's not just about one person it's two walking together to agree.

After being married and divorced I have learned and now understand so much in the Word of God. This has taken years of spiritual and natural maturity. I have such a great understanding of commitment, sacrifice, patience, peace, joy, dedication, and love. I have made detrimental emotional choices in my life. Until I started thinking just about me. Nobody else but me. Married and being in ministry and a leader, people looked up to me. I wore a mask for many years. I was so on fire for God, but miserable inside pretending to be happy and loved. I began seeing myself slowly change. I was not reading my Bible, studying, praying, or fasting. It was hard to stay on top of things. I was still going to church; I was in a shell ready to burst and was only thinking about myself. How can I get out of this and out of that? The devil can have you fooled thinking everything is ok. Imagine your life covered with a facade. I didn't trust anyone. I thought I could do everything on my own, until I had a nervous breakdown.

I found myself in a psychologist's office, and when they started asking me questions about my life, they wrote up an assessment and wanted to put me on medication. The spirit of God said to me what are you doing here? God had asked, Elijah the same thing when he was hiding in a cave—what are you doing here? I was in a mental cave within myself. Hearing God's voice made me realize, I had to depend on Him. I snapped out of what was happening to me. Then I knew I had to trust God and lean on Him for help. He healed my emotions a year later. It took so much fasting and praying and staying in the Word of God. But I am free today!

Looks Envied with All Hatred
Rachel may have had the looks that attracted Jacob, but she also had "looks envied with all hatred". The first letters of these words spell Leah. Rachel gave Bilhah to Jacob a second time. This relieved some of the pain and anguish she had for Leah. Genesis 30:8, "With great wrestling have I wrestled with my sister, and I have prevailed (and caught up with her)." If only Rachel understood the love Jacob had for her. As a woman, I get it. Children are a blessing from the Lord! A heritage from God and the fruit of the womb is His reward. Psalm 127:3-5 says, "Thy children like olive plants around the table." Psalm 128:3-4 says, "Under the law it was a shame for a woman not to have children as well as men."

How interesting it is that under the Talmud a husband could divorce his wife after ten years without having children, and guess what? The woman can remarry. Barrenness was curse, a punishment, according to Leviticus 20:21 and Jeremiah 22:30. Rachel wanted to die because it was a curse to be unfruitful and she experienced the embarrassment of not being able to carry the seed of her husband.

I believe when a person wants something so badly and they are anxious, paranoid, and frantic, it will hinder the flow of performance. Nothing was wrong with Jacob, it was Rachel. Has anyone ever thought about how Jacob felt? He had to put up with her nagging and the frustration of listening to her complain. To make matters worse, she blamed him. He was caught up as a pawn in Rachel and Leah's game.

They were racing to have children and wearing him out. Was there really a romance between these woman Jacob was involved with? In the midst of all the games they played, God brought forth the promises. God used their anger, resentment, jealousy, envy, hatred, unhappiness, and discouragement to accomplish His will. How many times in our past or present have women played games with men to get them to love them? Yes, even those who are saved and in the church. Let's talk about it because it's true. Some women would rather renounce their self-worth in Christ to get a man whether they are saved or not. They would do anything to get them and when they do, they realize it wasn't even worth it because of the hurt, embarrassment and guilt.

They didn't keep themselves pure and responded to their own fleshly needs. When you realize your worth as a woman, you will purposely value who you are, especially in Christ. Women who value themselves know that only Jesus truly loves them. Your husband can love you, but not the way Jesus can. Jesus will fill every void—mental, emotional, physical, and financial. He knows how to take care of you and gives restoration of the spirit, soul, and body.

Leah was in this place, when she gave birth to Judah, her fourth son. She said, "Now I will praise the Lord." Judah means praise! Judah was the tribe where Jesus bruised the head of the serpent. Leah knew one day there would be an end of her warring with her sister Rachel. Her dependency would be mainly on God! Leah knew that the Lord loved her because he opened her womb and was the first to give her husband children. Jesus' love supersedes all the emotions we have in our soul then he balances them, teaches us to control them, and soothes them with his healing. Take it from me I am a witness he will do it! Hallelujah!

A Continued Race

After Leah fourth's son was born, she continued to race ahead of Rachel in producing more children for Jacob. Genesis 30:9 says, "When Leah saw that she had left bearing, she took Zilpah her maid, and gave her to Jacob as wife." For a while Leah was producing well and bringing forth. And then there came a time that she couldn't have any more children. That tells me she had Jacob all to herself until she realizes she wasn't coming up pregnant anymore. Where was Rachel all this time? Leah was very selfish and controlling, she pushed to take the lead, and very resentful to Rachel. She was keeping Jacob all to herself.

That's what desperation will cause you to do to get someone to love you. You will find ways to hold on to a person. Let's keep in mind that Jacob was very patient. He waited for Rachel and had no true love for Leah. Jacob was in the polygamous state as a pawn but had just one love. I truly believe that Leah loved her husband dearly, but that love was not returned to her. I also believe Jacob loved her in some way, but differently than Rachel. Leah found a way to continue to give her husband children; it seems her love turned into lust. Lust is impatient while love is patient (Corinthians 13:4). She couldn't wait until she was fertile again. You see, lust takes, and love gives. Leah's passion for lust was demanding and so she decides to give her handmaid Zilpah to her husband to have more children.

What a trap Jacob was in. We see these games played all the time from both men and women. Remember this, it doesn't matter how old you are or how long you are saved, the devil's deception has not changed. When a woman or man tells you how bad they want you that's lust operating in full force! Lust gets what it wants, and Leah did just that using Zilpah. The handmaid bore another son and called him Gad. Genesis 30:11 says his name means a 'troop cometh'. Leah reinforced her position to stay in the lead and now has a 'little army'. Do you see how Leah was in control of this game?

The Mandrakes
In this scene Rachel still hasn't had children on her own. She asked for the mandrakes that she saw Reuben give to Leah, his mother. Mandrakes are flowering plants known as an aphrodisiac. They also are called the 'love apple' that helps put people in the mood romantically to enhance fertility.

I believe Leah prepared herself ahead of time with the mandrakes when she realized she would be Jacob's first wife, and this is the reason she bore his first four sons. The secret got out. Rachel saw her sister's little secret and desperately asked for of the plants. At this moment Rachel didn't care how she got them. She made a bargain with her sister in exchange for the mandrakes. The mandrakes were her last hope, or so she thought. It was in God's timing that He remembered Rachel and opened her womb. She brought forth her first child Joseph, which means "he will add". Her son Joseph was known as a type of

Christ. She received her child, and once she knew the secret, she wanted more. She wasn't satisfied. Dissatisfaction can bring more harm than good; in Rachel's case it ended her life.

Amazingly, Joseph had patience in everything he went through with his brothers. Rachel didn't have the spirit of patience to wait for God to move in her life. If I had known about Jesus early in my life, I would have waited until I was married to have children. We all learn from our mistakes and decisions. I am happy I have Jesus in my life today. I love my children dearly.

In Genesis 30:17-21 we see that God listened to Leah and in exchange for the mandrakes she brought Jacob two more sons and a daughter. Rachel's manipulation reversed because Leah got pregnant again after their agreement. Manipulation doesn't always go as planned. Rachel had no patience only desperation. Yet, God also listened to her in exchange for the mandrakes and this took away her reproach of barrenness of fertility.

There is a revelation associated with the mandrakes: God listened to Leah because she was wise (she devised a plan to use the mandrakes) and helped bring His plan to pass. Even though He didn't need the mandrakes, because Leah used the herbs in the earth, God honored it. All this time Rachel was barren until she saw Reuben giving his mom mandrakes. A light bulb went on in her mind. She thought *this will help me to become fertile*. God honored her request as well.

Rachel did not take into consideration the words of her mouth when she desired children so desperately; sadly, those words came to pass during the delivery of her second son Benjamin. We can say things that can be detrimental later without knowing. After Rachel's death, in the end Leah was the one who stood with Jacob. Leah was the strong one and loved her God. She understood where she was in her life with God. Leah is a great example for women who feel they are unattractive or not worthy to be with anyone. She was a great mother to Jacob's children, found favor, joy, peace within herself, and was faithful to both Jacob and God. In Him she found true love.

My advice to all women is love yourselves and see yourself the way that God sees you. It may be a struggle because it was with me growing up. That's ok. Stay with God and be faithful to Him. His love is greater than any other love in the world. The rewards are great. Blessings to you all.

References

What is the Difference between Gestational Artificial Insemination and Donor Surrogacy? By Mark Johnson March 24, 2014.

Website www.behindthename.com. 1996-2020 Mike Campbell.
Jewish News Rabbi Shulamit North London Reform Synagogue.
Jewish Virtual Library "Barrenness and Fertility"

The Bible Says What? 'A surrogate mother was cast out'
Genesis Chapter 29-30 Jon Courson Blue Letter Bible

Now Available on Amazon!

POWERED BY
L. RENEE RICHARDSON, MBA
KIM W. MILLER, B. S.
ELAINE ROBISON

BY
Fashioned GOD
TO RULE THE WORLD

A PowHERful Look at God's Original Design
for Womankind by 11 Women Leaders

A BOOK COLLABORATIVE

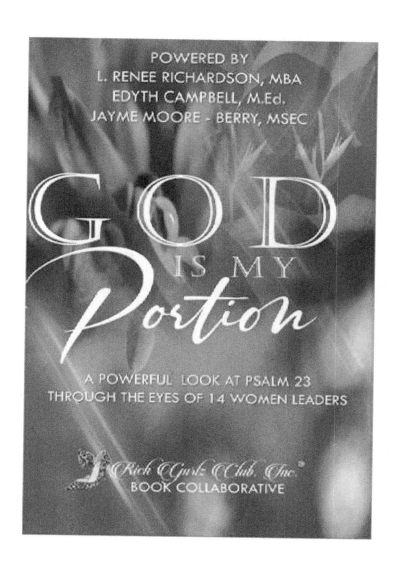

POWERED BY
L. RENEE RICHARDSON, MBA
EDYTH CAMPBELL, M.Ed.
JAYME MOORE - BERRY, MSEC

GOD
IS MY
Portion

A POWERFUL LOOK AT PSALM 23
THROUGH THE EYES OF 14 WOMEN LEADERS

Rich Gurlz Club, Inc.
BOOK COLLABORATIVE

101 GOD GIVEN *Kim*firmations

KIMBERLY J. OLIVER

A CHRIST CENTERED LEADERSHIP MODEL FOR TODAY'S LOCAL CHURCH

Coming Soon

***The Rich Gurlz Club is a Distinguished Partner and Supporter of
Women of Vision and Destiny Ministries Worldwide, Inc.***

About Women of Vision and Destiny Ministries Worldwide, Inc.

We are a PowerCircle™ of global women who educate,
empower and enlighten today's Christian women to impact the
world. We are philanthropists, international movers and shakers,
moms, and daughters. We lead nations, governments,
businesses, ministries, and corporations.

Our global headquarters is in the John Hancock Center Chicago
with regional Corporate Office and Dream CentHERS in
Columbus, GA. We have teams on three continents North
America, Asia and Africa. Our goal is to have TOP 2 Percent
LeadHERS on all 7 continents.

We believe in the power of the cluster anointing and mingle our God-inspired global grape juices to impact the lives of 4.0 billion women and young ladies across the globe. We are a hegemon-a global force for women in the world.

VISION

Our vision is to build 57 women's centers and 10 LOVED academies for young ladies in the U.S. and abroad on each continent. Our estimated cost is $4 billion.

Our WOVD TV presence is on 4 continents. North America, Australia, Africa and Asia.

WOVD was birthed on November 12, 2000 after a divine impartation into the life of our ordained Senior Pastor/Founder/CEO L. Renee Richardson, MBA, by Convening Apostle Dr. Ron Cottle of Columbus, GA. She has served in church leadership for 44 years. L. Renee grew up in the Columbus, GA Region graduating Magna Cum Laude from Columbus State University (BBA) and the University of Georgia (MBA). She was living in Chicago and was one of the top three women of color at one of the largest communications companies in the world at the time of the impartation. She left corporate America to open an ice cream store on Michigan Avenue with hubby Elder Glen Richardson.

Today L. Renee is the ChairHERman of the Board of three global corporations: Women of Vision and Destiny Ministries Worldwide, Inc., Wealth and Riches Today, Inc. and the I Am Worth It Foundation. She has an assignment to raise up the next generation of TOP 2 Percent Global Women Leaders.

On November 12, 2021, WOVD celebrates 21 years of educating, empowering and enlightening 1.5 million women and young ladies worldwide. Our foundational platform is WOVDU-the University of Life for Women which speaks to the hearts and minds of the 21st century woman. WOVDU provides spiritual guidance on issues related to being a Christian woman in her youth, college, the workforce, marriage, wealth, business ownership and spiritual enrichment and development.

Our WOVD flagship platform is the Power Up Your Faith Show which airs live Monday-Friday at 6 am cst/7 am est on WOVD TV (www.facebook.com/WOVDWW/Live). We spread Jesus 24/7 on the Good News Channel. On Oct. 1, 2020, Wealth and Riches Today, Inc. opened its WOVD Beautique featuring BlingBling apparel and nearly 100 SKUs at

www.wealthandrichestoday.com/SHOP.

WOVD offers different membership levels. Our signature membership is the WOVD PowerCircle 1001 Leading Ladies. Learn more about how you can join the sisterhood at www.powercircleinfo.eventbrite.com.

Miss Classy Christian BlingBling Apparel
1.6 Million Women's Lives Changed

$hopforCharity ProfitwithaPurpose

www.wealthandrichestoday.com/SHOP

Meet Miss Classy Christian our BlingBling Apparel that FUNraises for women and young ladies causes. HERstory is our story, our daughter's story, our sister's story and our mother's story. She struggled to get here but she did not give up. Our goal is to FUNraise to support 4 billion women worldwide.

This is our Signature Miss Classy Christian WOVD BlingBling Tee™.

Miss Classy Christian believes she has supernatural powers to touch the lives of women experiencing the toughest seasons of life. It is estimated that 1 in 3 women will face cancer. Many women are facing surmountable odds. In third world countries poverty is the norm. Miss Classy Christian enjoys showing up on the doorsteps of women on chemotherapy, stroke patients and nurses pressed beyond measure due to COVID.

Her desire is to bring the love of Jesus to women and take the sting out of debilitating diseases, poverty, abuse, unemployment, divorce, lack of education, imprisonments, discrimination, illiteracy, business failures, rape, molestation, and COVID. Her goal is to touch 4 billion plus women worldwide.

Miss Classy Christian brings joy, hope, warmth, love from the 1.3 million women worldwide WOVD has impacted over 21 years (November). She never gives up. She believes in the cluster anointing and desires for women to work together across the world. We are on 3 continents.

Miss Classy Christian is a BIG BODACIOUS dreamer who believes that God has big plans for her. Miss Classy Christian sales underwrite Women and Young Ladies Causes. Our WOVD Beautique's goal is to raise $1,000,001 plus annually.
Will you help us achieve this goal? Share this post. Buy 10 Miss Classy Christian products for your family and friends, women's group or women overcoming canHER.

#ShopforCharity! #EveryWoman. EveryWhere. EveryDay.

A Portion of Each Dollar Supports Women and Young Ladies Causes
- They are made in the U.S. by a Small Business
- Our WOVD BlingBling Tees have 1641 Rhinestones and Rhinestuds
- We pay a premium for additional cost to create design.
- They are custom made by robots.
- They come in many beautiful colors
- Sleeve Lengths: Long, Short, ¾ Sleeves
    - Collar Styles: V Neck, Round Neck and Crew Neck.
- Product Categories: Windbreakers, P3 Unlimited Blankets, Jackets, Tees, Baseball Tees, Jerseys, Acid Wash Pullovers
- Elements used: Emerald Rhinestones, Gold Studs, Purple Studs

- Design Size 9.40 in wide x 8.8 in tall
- 5.5 oz., 100% combed ring spun cotton jersey
  Heather is 93% cotton, 7% polyester
- Double-needle hemmed sleeves and bottom
- Softly shaped for a classic, feminine fit

Made in the USA
Monee, IL
05 November 2021